COLLINS
COBUILD

COLLINS Birmingham University International Language Database

English Course

Jane & Dave Willis

Student's Book

1

Collins ELT
8 Grafton Street
London W1X 3LA

COBUILD is a trademark of William Collins Sons & Co. Ltd

© William Collins Sons & Co. Ltd 1988

10 9 8 7 6 5 4 3 2

First published 1988
Reprinted 1988

Printed in Hong Kong by Wing King Tong Company Ltd

ISBN 0 00 370026 7

Design: Snap Graphics
Cover design: Richard Morris
Photography: Chris Ridgers
Artwork: Jonathan Allen, Sarah Allison, Laura Boyd, Lynn Breeze, David Brown, Terry Burton, William Cherno, Ian Dicks, Doges Design, Eric Kincaid, Mike Mosedale, Mark Owen, Val Sangster, Paul Shorrock, Clive Spong, Andrew Wright

This Student's Book is accompanied by a set of cassettes ISBN 0 00 370029 1, a Practice Book ISBN 0 00 370027 5, and a Teacher's Book ISBN 0 00 370028 3. A booklet containing transcripts of the unscripted recordings is included inside the back cover of the Student's Book.

COBUILD is the Collins Birmingham University International Language Database

Acknowledgements *(Figures in brackets refer to sections.)*

The syllabus of the Collins COBUILD English Course is based on the research findings of the COBUILD project at Birmingham University. Editor-in-Chief: Professor John Sinclair.

Liaison between COBUILD and Collins was co-ordinated by Antoinette Renouf. A special team prepared data for Level 1: Christopher Greaves, Stephen Heap, Ann Hewings (who also helped compile the 'Grammar Book') and Rosemary Thompson. Computer support was provided by Tim Lane.

The authors would especially like to thank the COBUILD team listed above, Ron Carter, for advice on the lexical syllabus, and comments on early units, and Michael Halliday for guidance on the Grammar material. They are also grateful to teachers and students at the British Council, Singapore, and the British Council students at the Japanese Association of Singapore who carried out early trialling of the material. Finally, the authors would like to thank family and friends, especially their daughters, Jenny and Becky, for all their help and patience throughout the writing of this book.

Many people read and commented on the manuscript and it is impossible to list them all here. The publishers and authors are especially grateful to the following: Rosie Allen, Alistair Banton, Sarah Crothers, Tony Duff, Anthony Forrester, Margaret Hanson, Jenny McAslan, Georgina Pearce, Hilary Rees-Parnall and Paula Walker.

The publishers and authors would like to thank the following teachers and institutions who tested draft material and/or provided valuable feedback: *Algeria*: Saïd Alim; Saâdia Taharbouchet. *Greece*: Patrick McGavigan (Centre for Applied Language Learning, Athens). *Hong Kong*: The British Council. *Indonesia*: The British Council, Bandung. *Italy*: The British Council, Naples; IPC Fortunato, Naples. *Japan*: The British Council, Kyoto. *People's Republic of China*: Shanghai Foreign Language Institute. *Spain*: I.B. Camilo Jose Cela, Padrón. *Thailand*: Pathum Thani Agricultural Campus, Institute of Technology and Vocational Education. *UK*: Bedford English Study Centre; Centre of English Language Teaching, University of Warwick; Chichester College of Technology; Christopher Hare (Filton Technical College, Bristol); International House, London; Pamela Vickers (Polytechnic of Central London/South East London College). *West Germany*: British Council, Munich; Judith Port Fox, Frankfurt am Main.

The following participated in the unscripted recordings, and provided supporting texts and information to ensure the contextualisation of the recordings was accurate: Bob Bushaway, Christopher Collier-Wright, David Foll, Bridget Green, Philip King, Danny Lim, Ken O'Connell, Charles Owen, Sue Purseglove, Myf Sinclair and Jenny Vaughan. We are also grateful to the many others who helped with or participated in recordings for the Course, and especially to Martin Williamson, for producing the recordings and for his advice throughout.

Most of those in the published recordings also gave time to be photographed, as did the following: William Glason ('Chris'), Alan Hancock ('Charles'), Pippa Higham (140), Katie Mackenzie-Stuart (33), Martin Mulloy (33). The following allowed us to take photographs at their premises: Bournville College of Further Education (109), Eurocentres – Davies's School of English, London SW1 (152), Lillywhites, London W1 (187), Nisa Supermarket, London W8 (152, 188), Westminster College, London W1.

The publishers are grateful to the following for permission to use original material in the Student's Book: British Railways Board for part of Young Person's Railcard application form (14) and timetable extract (225); Eurocentres – Davies's School of English, London SW1; The English Language Centre Bristol; The International School, Exeter for extracts from enrolment forms (14); Guinness Superlatives Ltd 1987 for extracts adapted from *Guinness Book of Records 1986* (18, 55); *Portland Town* (Derroll Adams) © 1964, Planetary–Nom (London) Ltd, c/o 45 Berkeley Square, London W1X 5DB (69); Reader's Digest and Valerie Ball (74); Christian Brann Ltd, Phoenix Way, Cirencester, Glos. for extracts from *Pass the Port* (74, 91); BBC World Service for extract from *London Calling* (77); British Airways plc for part of boarding card (77); Cheselbourne Community Fund for raffle ticket (77); Regent School of English, 19–23 Oxford Street, London W1R 1RF for parts of their prospectus (82, 179); Just Seventeen, EMAP Metro Publications for extracts and photographs (98, 163, 225); BBC English by Radio for logo (146); Andrea Drayton for diary extract (151); Reader's Digest and Janet Morgan (160); Reader's Digest and Harold Smith (161); Reader's Digest and G. T. Parker (173); Brad Anderson/Masters Agency, Jerry Marcus/Good Housekeeping, and Bryan Reading for cartoons (173); British Tourist Authority for extract from *Britain, London Map* (179); Department of Tourism, York 'Living History' for extract from *Where to Stay 1985* (179); Western Publishing Company Inc. for extract from *Golden Geographic Encyclopaedia* © 1958 (179); PA NewsFeatures, Fleet Street, London for extract from article on Tina Turner (190); British Council, John Swales, John Merritt, Dr Tickoo for letters and telex (193); British Telecom for extracts from *The Phone Book* and *Welcome to Britain* (205, 206); Reader's Digest and E. Lee (210); Zambia National Tourist Board for extracts, map (adapted) and photograph from *Tourist Map of Zambia* (221); Radio Times (225); Ted Rodgers (230); Reader's Digest and Richard Kopplin (232); Shreveport Times (232); Ruth Johnson (233); Julian Cooke (JC), Liz Fotheringham (EF) and Becky Willis (BW) (various texts).

The publishers are grateful to the following for the use of photographs: Barnaby's Picture Library (18, 49, 55, 67, 82, 96, 113, 142, 151, 155, 175, 176, 187, 191); BBC Hulton Picture Library (46); Britain on View (BTA/ETB) (155, 178, 187, 225); British Council © 1984 (187); British Council, Singapore (193); Colorific! (55, 72, 191); Colorsport (77); Julian Cooke (157); Mary Evans Picture Library (165); Flatt and Mead Estate Agents, Hemel Hempstead (58); The Image Bank (77, 96, 191); Macmillan Publishers Ltd (146); Oxfam/Camilla Garrett Jones (104); Oxfam (104); Van Phillips (170); The Photographer's Library (18, 148, 191); Pictor International, London (55); Picturepoint, London (96, 135, 187, 191); Picturepoint/Lancaster University (135); Rank Travel (170); Fergus Sinclair (221); Spectrum Colour Library (18, 49, 108, 155, 170, 187, 225); Tony Stone Photolibrary, London (18, 221); Thomson Cities (171); Topham (96, 190); Jane and Dave Willis (223).

Contents

OK. Can you give me your address?

1 Hello

1 Who says what?

a Hello.
Hi.

Good morning. I'm James Barnes. I'm from ICG.
Hello.

b I'm Mrs Fish. Anna Fish. You can call me Anna.

c Laura, this is Mario.
Nice to meet you.
And you.

d Goodbye, see you on Monday.
Bye!

e Who's that?
I don't know.

2 Do you know...?

Read and answer.

Do you know your teacher's name?
No./Yes, it's _____ .

Do you know the names of the students next to you?
Yes/No.

Do you know the names of the students in your class?
Yes/No.

Do you know where they're from?
Yes/No.

Tell the student next to you your name.
Tell him or her where you're from.

Tell the class about the student next to you.

Write down the names of the students next to you.

3 A–Z

Do you know the names of the letters in English?
Say these letters.

Where do these letters go?

m e y h
g q

4 People to listen to

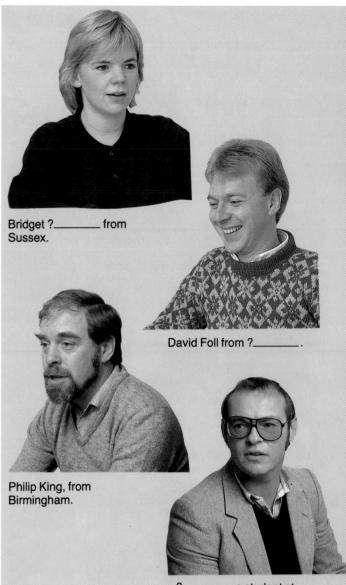

Bridget ?_____ from Sussex.

David Foll from ?_____ .

Philip King, from Birmingham.

?_____ , a student at Birmingham.

4a a   What's Bridget's surname?
Where's David from?
Who's Chris? What's his surname?

4b b   Who are the people on the tape?
What are their surnames?
Write down their full names.

c   Write the letter T if the sentence is *true*, or the letters NT if it's *not true*.

For example, the first sentence, 1, is *true* so you write T.

1 *David's surname is Foll.*
2 *He's from Birmingham.*
3 *Bridget's surname is Green.*
4 *She's from London.*
5 *Philip King is from Birmingham.*
6 *His first name is Philip.*
7 *We don't know Chris's first name.*
8 *He's a student at Birmingham.*

Write four (4) true sentences about Bridget and David.

Write three (3) true sentences about the student next to you.

5 First names, middle names, surnames

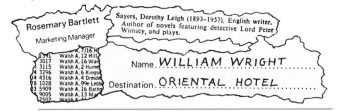

Names in English

In Britain most people have three names, a first name, a middle name, and a surname. People don't use their middle names much.

People never use Mr, Mrs, or Miss with their first names. You can't say 'Miss Bridget', for example. You can only say 'Miss Green'. Miss goes with the surname, Green, not with the first name, Bridget.

British people say their first names first and their surnames last. It's not the same as in Chinese, for example – Chan Guo Ming, a Chinese student, says his surname, Chan, first.   JRW

5 We talked to some students about their names. This is what one of them said.

My name's Eleni Andreou. I'm from Athens. Eleni is my first name. In Athens, most people call me 'Kyria Eleni'. ('Kyria' means 'Mrs'.) But in England, people call me 'Mrs Andreou'. EA

Ask other people.

How do you say your name in your country?

Do you say your surname first, as in Chinese? Yes/No.

Do you say Mr or Mrs or Miss with your first name? Yes/No.

What do your friends call you?

6 Numbers 1–12

a Do you know the numbers in English?
Look at these numbers. Which numbers are missing?

b Say which numbers are missing.

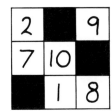

c Play Bingo!

Read this and do what it says.

Write either two or five.
Write either four or nine.
Write either ten or three.
Either seven or eleven.
Either six or eight.
Either one or twelve.

Cross out the numbers your teacher says like this:

When all your numbers are finished, say Bingo!

Which student was first to finish?

 Play Bingo again.

7 Puzzle

This is a triangle: a b c

How many triangles are the same?
How many triangles are different?

How many triangles are there here?

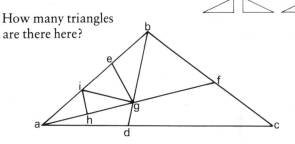

Write down all the triangles you can see, like this:

a b d, ahi, ghi

You have one minute!

Read out the letters of one triangle to the class. How many different triangles did the whole class find?

8 *Language study*

's, is, 're, are

Read these examples. They are all from Unit 1. Find all these words: **'s, is, 're, are**.

1 What does **'s** mean?
2 When do we say **is** (or **'s**) and when do we say **are** (or **'re**)?

Who's that?

Do you know where they're from?
Tell him or her where you're from.

This is _____. She's from _____.

Where's David from?
Who's Chris? What's his surname?
Who are these people? What are their surnames?

9 Phone numbers

9a **a** Chris asks Philip for his phone number. Write it down.

9b **b** David asks Bridget for her phone number, then Bridget asks David for his number. Write the numbers down.

c Read this and do what it says.

> Ask four students for their names and phone numbers. Write them down, and then check you have written them correctly.

10 Addresses

Read these addresses.

There are three mistakes on David Foll's letter, two mistakes on Philip King's letter, and one on Bridget Green's parcel.

10 Find four of the mistakes.

For example, the number is wrong on David's letter. It says 23, but on the tape David says 21.

First David asks Bridget for her address, and then Bridget asks David for his address.

Then Philip tells Chris his address.

Check your answers with your partner.

12 Classroom language

12

S: *Sorry, I don't understand this.*

S: *Sorry, can you say that again?*
T: *Yes, of course.*

11 Language study

Asking for addresses and phone numbers

11 First read the questions below and then listen. David, Bridget, Chris and Philip use eight of these questions. Which questions do they use?

What's your phone number?
Have you got a phone number?
And your phone number?
Have you got a phone? What's your number, then?

Can you give me your address?
Could you give me your address?
Can I have your address?
What's the postcode?

Sorry, could you repeat that?
Sorry, how do you spell that?
Can you spell your name for me?
Can you tell me how you spell your name?

13 English sounds

There are four sets of words here. Say them to your partner.
All the words in set 1 have the same sound in them. Which sound? What about sets 2, 3 and 4?

1 road, okay, phone, don't, know, hello, no
2 I'm, my, five, nine, right, why, Y
3 three, south, north
4 the, this, these, they

13 Say the words again after the tape.

14 Understanding forms

Look at these forms. What are they for? Which one is different?

A

Learn English in England
Reply coupon for further information. To:

The International School,
Exeter, Devon,
EX2 4EW, England.

Please send me information and registration forms for your English courses.
(Please write in CAPITAL letters)

My age is .... My level of English is: Advanced/Intermediate
(if under 21) Elementary/No English

My name is ....

My address is ....

....

Town .... Country ....

B

Enrolment Form

Please print or type

☐ Mrs. ☐ Miss ☐ Mr.

DAVIES'S
SCHOOLS OF ENGLISH

Surname

First name

Street

Town   Postal code

Country _____ Tel. No. at home
_____ Tel. No. at work

C

YOUNG PERSON'S RAILCARD
APPLICATION FORM

Mr/Mrs/Miss/Ms (Surname)_____ Initials_____

Home Address_____

_____

_____ Postcode_____

Please tick box if you are a student_____ ☐

D

Application for Enrolment

To: The Secretary,
The English Language Centre Bristol,
44 Pembroke Road, Bristol BS8 3DT.

Family name Mr/Mrs/Miss _____

First name(s) _____

Nationality _____

Home address _____

_____

Telephone number _____

My level of English is:

Beginner ☐ Elementary ☐ Intermediate ☐ Advanced ☐

If you are a beginner can you read and write the letters of the English Alphabet?

Yes ☐ No ☐

Choose one of these forms. Ask another student for their name, address etc., and write down the answers on your form. Then ask the student to check what you have written.

15 *Language study*

Look at the full stops (.) and commas (,) in the forms. Do you use full stops and commas in the same way in your language?

16 Meeting people you don't know

Look at the pictures. Who is saying what? What do you think they will say next?

A: *Who's that with Richard?*
B: *I don't know.*

    C: *Hello, my name's Elizabeth.*
    D: *Hi, I'm Richard. I'm from Newtown Computers. And you?*

E: *Dave, this is Sue, Sue Jones from Manchester. Sue, meet my husband, Dave.*
F: *Hello.*
G: *Hello, Sue, nice to meet you.*

A: *Ah, Good morning! Mrs Kent? My name's Johnson. Please come in.*
B: *Good morning Mr Johnson. Yes. I'm Amy Kent, from KCC.*

A: *Come and meet my secretary, June. June, this is Mrs Kent, director of KCC.*
C: *How do you do, Mrs Kent.*
B: *How do you do, June.*

16 Find out what they say after this.

a Words for people

Find the word that is not a person.

> teacher, students, partner, person, people, friend, secretary, director, number, man, woman, I, you, he, she, they

b Words for things you can write

Find two things you can't write.
e.g. You can write an *address* but not a *triangle*.

> word, name, number, address, letters of the alphabet, triangle, question, answer, telephone

c Words for names

Which two mean the same?

> first name, middle name, surname, full name, family name

d Words for words

> word, phrase, sentence

e What can you do with a word

Find the word that is wrong.
e.g. You can *say* a word, but you can't _____ a word.

> say, know, write, repeat, read, look at, find, listen to, come, spell

f his, her?

Is Sue his friend or her friend?
Is this his office or her office?
Is June his secretary or her secretary?

g and

🔲 17g How do you say these phrases?

Bridget and David. | Bridget, David and Philip.
Name and address. | Name, address and phone number.
Come and meet June. | Come and see June.
Can you read and write the English alphabet?
Come and sit down. | Go and sit down.
Monday and Wednesday. | Monday, Wednesday and Friday.

h Days of the week

Do you know the names of the days?

> *Weekdays:* Monday, Tuesday, Wednesday, Thursday, Friday
> *Weekend:* Saturday, Sunday

i When?

a.m. or p.m.?

> morning, afternoon, evening

Bye! See you Friday evening
Bye bye, Anne!

j is, are

How many people? One or two?

Bridget is English. She's from Sussex.
David is English. He's from London.
Bridget and David are English. They're not from Birmingham.
Are you from England or America?
You're English.

k of

🔲 17k How do you say the word **of** in these sentences?

Do you know the names of the students in your class?
What's the name of your road?
Do you know the names of the days of the week in English?
Do you know the letters of the English alphabet?
In groups of four.
The London School of English.
She's the director of KCC.
How many examples of the word 'of' are there in these sentences?

l know

Do you know David?
I don't know London.
I know 91 words in English.

m can

Can I have your address, please?
Can you give me your address?
Can you give me your phone number?
Can you say that again please?

n come

Come in!
She comes from London.
Come and meet my friend.

Important words to remember (91 so far)

address	first	letter	of	six	two
am	five	London	one	student	use
and	form	look	or	Sunday	Wednesday
are	four	me	page	surname	what
ask	Friday	meet	people	teacher	where
book	friend	Miss	person	tell	who
can	from	Monday	phone	ten	word
class	goodbye	Mr	photograph	this	write
come	he	Mrs	please	three	yes
day	hello	my	read	Thursday	you
different	her	name	same	today	your
eight	his	nice	Saturday	tomorrow	
either	I	nine	say	tonight	
eleven	is	no	secretary	true	
English	know	not	seven	Tuesday	
example	learn	number	she	twelve	

Biggest family in the world
Feodor Vassilyev (1707–82), from
Shuya, 150 miles east of Moscow, and
his first wife: 69 children.

Biggest family in Great Britain
Elizabeth, wife of John Mott, married in
1676, of Monks Kirby, Warwickshire
had 42 children. She died in 1720.

Great Britain's champion mothers of
today are Mrs Margaret NcNaught
(b.1923) of Birmingham (12 boys and
10 girls), and Mrs Mabel Constable
(b.1920) of Long Itchington,
Warwickshire, who has also had 22
children . . .

18 | Families and family trees

Think of someone you know. What do you know
about their family?
Which of these sentences are true?

_____ has got
    one brother
    a brother and a sister
    just one sister
    no brothers or sisters
    a sister and two brothers
    a brother and two sisters
    two sisters
    two brothers
    a lot of brothers
    a lot of sisters
    a lot of brothers and sisters

_____
    isn't married
    is married and has two children
    is married but has no children
    is married and has one child
    is married and has three children
    is married and has more than three children

Look at the photographs above. Whose family trees
are these?

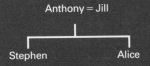

11

19 Bridget and David's families

John
Paul
David

Jane
Pat
Felicity
Sarah
Emma

a David tried to find out about Bridget's family. Draw Bridget's family tree. Fill in the names.

19b **b** Bridget asked David about his family. Draw David's family tree. Fill in the names.

Rosemary
Anthony
Bridget
Richard
Sheila

19c **c** David tried to remember the names of Bridget's family, and then Bridget tried to remember David's family.
Which of them had the better memory?

d Look at the names again. Which are girls' names and which are boys' names?

---

20 *Language study*

a have got

Look at these examples from the recordings of Bridget and David.

There are no full stops (.) or question marks (?).

1 Which examples are questions?
2 What is the word **'ve**?
3 Which words come before and after **got**?

DF: Have you got any brothers and sisters
BG: Yes, I've got one sister called Rosemary
DF: Okay

BG: And have they got any children
DF: Mhm. Two children, two girls
BG: Yes

BG: and you've got one sister called Felicity
DF: Mhm

BG: And they've got two daughters called . . . Emma and . . .
DF: Sarah
BG: Sarah
DF: Mm

20 **b** Listen and repeat each phrase. Then practise saying some of these phrases with your partner. Listen for two stresses in each group of words.

*Have you got any **brothers** and **sisters**?*
*I've got **one** sister called **Rosemary**.*
Two children.
Two girls.

---

21 *Classroom language*

21 Practise these dialogues. When could you use them?

S1: *Sorry, I can't remember your name.*
S2: *Petra.*
S1: *Thanks.*

S1: *Er, excuse me, that's my pen!*
S2: *Oh, I'm sorry.*
S1: *It's okay!*

S1: *Shall we start?*
S2: *Just a minute! . . . Right.*

S1: *So we've finished . . .*
S2: *That's it, yes.*

Find the words **start, finish, sorry** and **remember**. When can you use them?

12

22 Your partner's family

How good are you at names?
Tell your partner about your family.

Either **or**

If you're not married, start with your parents, and then go on to your brothers and sisters.

If you are married, start with your brothers and sisters, and then go on to your husband or wife and children.

Write the names of your partner's family on a family tree.

How many names can you remember? Don't look at your partner's family tree!

Which of you has the better memory?

> Now write some sentences about your family. Then write some sentences about your partner's family. Give your sentences to your partner to read and check.

23 Useful things

 a Which words in the list go with which picture?

b Which things from the list have you got with you today? Tell your partner.

Has your partner got the same things? How many things have you *both* got?

List

a pen
a pencil
some money
a credit card
an address book
a watch
a calculator
some keys
a driving licence
an identity card
some tissues
a ten pence coin

> Tell the class which things you have both got.
> First plan what you are going to say.

Which pair gave the longest list?

24 Danny and Jenny

a Read about Danny and Jenny. Say which picture is Danny's office and which picture is Jenny's office.

Danny lives in London. He's self-employed[1]. He's got a studio office in Holborn in central London, where he works with his brother.

They have a design agency. 'We do leaflets, brochures, . . . that sort of thing. So we're both self-employed, both me and my brother.'

They also have a 'rep'[2], somebody who goes out and finds more work for them.

Jenny is also self-employed. She's an editor and writer. She works for a lot of different companies.

Jenny has a flat in North London and she works from home: 'I've got a sort of office in my flat . . .'   JC

[1] self-employed = he doesn't have a boss; he's his own boss.
[2] 'rep' = representative.

b True, or not true?

1 *Danny and Jenny both live in London.*
2 *Danny and his brother both work in the same office.*
3 *They are both self-employed.*

4 *Jenny's also self-employed.*
5 *She has a 'rep' who finds work for her.*
6 *Jenny hasn't got an office.*
7 *She's a writer.*

24c **c** Write down Danny and Jenny's full names.

25 Danny and Jenny's things

We asked Danny and Jenny to do the same as you did in section 23.
What things do you think *both* of them had with them? Write down four things.

25 Find out what things both of them had.
Make a table like this one.

	Jenny	Danny
a pen		
a pencil		
money		
a credit card		
an address book		
a watch		

Did they have the same things as you and your partner?

26 More men than women?

26a **a** Danny and Jenny tried to find out if they had more men than women in their families.
How many men are there in Danny's family?
How many women are there in his family?
What about Jenny's family?

26b **b** David and Bridget did the same. How many men and boys do they have in their families, and how many women and girls?

Check with your partner. Have you got the same answers?

27 *Language study*

a has got

27a These examples are from the recording of Bridget and David in section 26b.
Some of the full stops (.) and question marks (?) are missing. Say where they go.

DF: So what about – let's go back to your family tree.
BG: Right. How about your father Has he got any brothers or sisters
DF: Mm – got one brother, one sister
BG: And your mother
DF: Just one sister

1 Why do they say **has** and not **have**?
2 What word is **'s** here? – *She's got . . .*
3 What do **Right** and **Mm** mean?

b What about . . .?

When do we say **What about . . .?**
Is **How about . . .?** the same?

c Now practise saying some of these phrases with your partner.

28 Class family survey

What about your families? How many women and girls are there in your partner's family, and how many men and boys?

Ask about brothers and sisters, then about parents' brothers and sisters, and then children.

Fill in a Survey Form like this one.

Student name	Men/boys	Women/girls	Totals
(you)			
(partner)			

▶ Tell the class about your partner's family. First plan carefully what to say, and write it down. ◀

Listen to the other students. Write down the numbers of men and women in their families.
In all your families together, are there more men and boys or women and girls?

29 *Language study* ··············

Words ending in s

Look at the transcripts below of David and Bridget talking about their families (sections 26b and 19).

How many words are there ending in **s** or **'s**?
Does the **s** or **'s** always mean the same?

Some words always end in **s**, for example, **his**.

What about this one?

*I've got one brother and **he's** got two daughters.*

Put the words ending in **s** or **'s** into 4 categories.

Bridget's family
DF: If we look at, erm, your mother Sheila. Has she got any brothers and sisters?
BG: Yes, she's got one sister.
DF: No brothers?
BG: No.
DF: Okay. What about your father?
BG: He's got three sisters.
DF: Oh, and no brothers?
BG: No.

David's family
BG: Now it's my turn. Your father's called John? and your mother's called Pat? –
DF: That's right.

BG: and your brother's married – to . . . Jane?
DF: Jane. Good.
BG: Jane. And they've got two daughters called . . . Emma and – Sarah.

Now look at the text in section 24. Find thirteen more words that end in **s** and put them into categories.

30 English sounds ··············

a Say these words to your partner. Which sound is in all of them?

> number, London, mother, brother, one, young, Sunday, Monday, company

30a Say the words again.

30b **b** Listen for the sounds that are not stressed, like the -er in **sister**. Which other words have the same -er sound?

Have you got any brothers and sisters?
I've got a sister called Rosemary.
What are your parents called?
Sheila and Richard.
What about her friend Sarah?
She's older than me.
She works for a computer company.

c Now practise saying the phrases.

Say two sentences like these about yourself and your partner.

31 Asking for something

31 Which dialogue do you think goes with the picture?
Listen and then practise these dialogues with your partner.

A: *Excuse me, have you got Liz's phone number?*
B: *Sorry, no, not on me. I've got it at home.*
A: *Oh, never mind! Thanks, anyway.*
B: *Bye!*

> A: *Excuse me, have you got a 10p coin?*
> B: *Just a minute, yes. Here.*
> A: *Thank you very much.*
> B: *That's okay.*

15

a Words for people

Put these words into 3 lists:

men/boys women/girls either

Write them down.

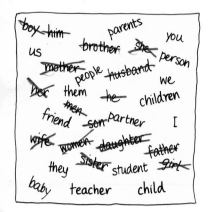

b got

I've got you've got we've got they've got	your book a pen a calculator some tissues
he's got she's got	my keys some money

Have you got Have I got Have they got Has he got Has she got	your things? your pen? their keys? a 10p coin? any money?

c have, has

I have you have we have they have	a small baby a big family four children

Green has ord has as has	an office in London. six credit cards. a big Mercedes.

d things

*How many things? One thing.
Two things.
Which things? My things.
Which people have the same
things?
some useful things
a list of things: pen, pencil,
calculator . . .
The first thing to remember is –
speak English!*

e How many?

One or more than one?

/s/ or /z/ or /ɪz/?

	thing key book student friend address watch family company baby		things keys books students friends addresses watches families companies babies
a an		some	
	person child man woman		people children men women

f my/our   your

my family   your family
our families   your families

his/her/their

his family, her family
their families

g a, an

We say 'a name' but
'an address', 'a
young man' but 'an
old man'. Why?

h both, also/too

*We've both got our keys.
I've also got my keys.
David's got his keys, too.*

*Danny's self-employed.
Jenny's also self-employed.
They both work in London.*

*We both had a pen, some money
and some keys.*

*We also had our calculators./We
had our calculators, too.*

*What things do you think both of
them had with them?*

i Things you do in class

*Listen and write the names . . .
Read about Jenny and Danny.
Find out about your partner's
family.
Ask them about their family.
Tell them about your family.
Tell the class about your
partner's family.
Plan carefully what to say.
Write two sentences.
Can you remember their names?
I can't remember!*

j Things people say

Excuse me!	Yes.
Sorry!	Yeah.
Thank you.	Okay? (OK?)
That's okay (OK).	Okay. (OK.)
That's all right.	

---

address am and are ask book can class come day different eight either eleven English example first five form four Friday friend from goodbye he hello her his I is know learn letter London look me meet Miss Monday Mr Mrs my name nice nine no not number of one or page people person phone photograph please read same Saturday say secretary seven she six student Sunday surname teacher tell ten this three Thursday today tomorrow tonight true Tuesday twelve two use Wednesday what where who word write yes you your about any baby big both boy brother but call carefully child daughter family father find finish get girl had have how husband it key list listen lot man many married mean money more mother office okay old our parent picture plan remember right shall sister

Important words to remember (155 so far)

about	daughter	it	mother	shall	they
any	family	key	office	sister	thing
baby	father	list	okay	small	useful
big	find	listen	old	so	we
both	finish	lot	our	son	which
boy	get	man	parent	sorry	wife
brother	girl	many	picture	start	woman
but	had	married	plan	stop	yeah
call	have	mean	remember	talk	young
carefully	how	money	right	thank	
child	husband	more	section	their	

even experience farm forest France happen here high hill history hot idea later let mountain never perhaps possible pretty put rain reason river roof run Scotland sea season single sky spring state summer sun suppose top type weather will winter above again arrangement arrive been below future lose receive should soon therefore understand whether available daily emergency especially fire free hear help if instruction keep machine necessary power private public service situation speak telephone whatever while within air chance figure holiday hope however love miss set since towards

33 Colours

What colour are:

    the man's jeans?
    the man's shoes?
    the woman's shoes?
    the woman's glasses?

What colour is:

    the woman's coat?
    the woman's blouse?
    the man's shirt?
    the man's hair?
    the woman's hair?
    her skirt?
    her bag?

What about the other things in the picture?

Now close your books. How much can you remember? Say things like this.

The man's hair is brown.

17

34 Where's the blue one?

on the left
on the right
in the middle
next to the red one
on the right of the red one
on the left of the black one
between the red one and the orange one

True or not true?

a The red phone is in the middle.
b The green one is next to the red one.
c The orange phone is between the blue one and the white one.
d The yellow one is to the left of the black one.
e The yellow one is to the left of the red one.
f The white one is on the right.
g The green phone is next to the black one.
h The black one is between the green one and the yellow one.
i The green one is on the left.
j The blue phone is between the black one and the yellow one.

35 What shapes are there?

a Read these sentences. Are they *true* or *not true*?

1 *There are a lot of different shapes.*
2 *There are some black ones.*
3 *There are also some brown ones.*
4 *Some of the black shapes are squares.*
5 *Some of the yellow ones are squares.*
6 *There are two blue squares.*
7 *There are six red shapes altogether.*
8 *There are two white shapes.*
9 *Both the white shapes are triangles.*
10 *There are four black shapes.*
11 *All the black shapes are squares.*
12 *None of the yellow shapes are squares.*
13 *There are more green shapes than red ones.*
14 *There are more green triangles than black ones.*
15 *Neither of the white shapes is a square.*
16 *There's only one big blue square.*
17 *There are twenty-five shapes altogether.*

35b b All the sentences on the tape are true. Practise saying them.

35c c Repeat the short phrases.

36 Same or different?

a Look at these two pictures. Are they the same or different?
How many differences can you find?

36b b How many differences did David and Bridget find?

c Write a list of the things that are different. For example:

brown hair/fair hair

d Then write sentences like this.

> *In one picture, the girl has got brown hair, but in the other picture she's got fair hair.*

18

36b **a** When does David say these things?

DF: Okay, so that's a difference.

DF: Okay, that's another one.

DF: So that's a third one.

DF: Ah, there's another one. That's four.

b Is the girl wearing an orange blouse? How does David describe it?

Look at the pictures. What things could you describe as:

sort of reddish	sort of yellowy brown
greeny blue	dark brown
bluish	light blue

---

38 # Find the differences

a Group A look at the picture on page 99. Group B look at the picture on page 100.

Talk to the people in your group about your picture.

What questions can you ask someone from the other group about their picture?

Get into pairs, each student from group A with a student from group B. Don't show your picture to your partner!

Each talk about your own picture and find the differences.

▶ How many differences did you find? Tell the class. ◀

38b **b** How many differences did Danny and Jenny find? Which ones did they miss?

---

a **Identifying people**

Find the phrases that tell you which person Danny and Jenny are talking about.

On the far left, I've got a woman.

And the man in the middle of the picture has ...

And the woman on the right has ...

The woman next to him has ...

b **Describing people**

What words and phrases come after **is**?

How many ways are there of describing people? (For example, you can talk about their clothes, their ...)

The girl on the left is wearing a sort of orangey blouse.

She has got fair hair.

The lady in my picture is blonde.

Next comes a man with blonde hair and a brown hat.

And the third woman has sort of reddish hair.

She is carrying a pink bag and wearing a grey skirt.

40a **a** Each of these three sets has one sound in common. For example, all the words in set 1 have a /k/ sound in them. What about the other sets?

1 colour, black, clothes, square, coin, look

2 grey, wearing, right, brown, address, different

3 yellow, glasses, light, blue, middle, little

40b **b** What about the letter **r** in these words? Can you hear it?

are, arm, car, partner, shirt, her, were, word, teacher, picture, water

c Read this, and say which is the key word in each phrase.

A: *Which one would you like? The small blue Ford?*

B: *No, the big blue Ford.*

A: *What about the big red Ford?*

B: *No, the large blue Ford.*

A: *Not the small blue Fiat?*

B: *NO! The large blue Ford!*

40c Listen and see if you were right. (One phrase has two stressed words. Which one?)

19

41 Classroom language

41

S: *Why does Bridget say 'reddish', not 'red'?*
T: *Well, 'reddish' hair means not very red, a bit brown ...*

S: *Why is it 'Are there', not 'There are'?*
T: *Because it's a question.*
S: *Oh, I see.*

S: *Why is there an 's' in the word 'colours'?*
T: *Because there's more than one colour.*
S: *Oh, thanks.*

42 Game

What was there on the tray?

a Look at the picture on page 84. How many things are there on the tray?

Look at the tray for one minute. Then see how many things you can remember.

42b **b** Look at page 84 and listen to Danny. How many things did he remember? How many things did he forget?

42c **c** Jenny tells Danny how many things he forgot. Were you right?

d Now don't look at the tray. Can you say where all the things were? For example:

The bananas were on the left.
The ruler was between the glasses and the glass of water.

43 Wordpower

light

How many different meanings has the word **light** got here?

Shall we have the light on?
Can you turn the lights off, please?
The lights were red.
There's a green light – lets go!
Shall I light the gas?

A: Shall I carry that for you?
B: No thanks – it's very light.

She had a light blue shirt on and dark trousers.

44 Language study

there

Look at this example from the recording. What words come after **there**?

DL: Below the bananas ... was [...] a notebook. And there was something above that but I can't remember. Erm ... Then there were some coins on the right-hand side of the book.

Look at section 35. What words come after **there**?

Look at the questions below. Where do the words **was** and **are** come? Why?

What was there on the tray?
How many things are there on the tray?

45 Grammar words

There is (There's), There are

Look at the coloured square in section 35. Make sentences from this table.

There are	two blue squares.
	a big blue triangle on the left.
There is	more green shapes than red ones.
	a blue square to the left of the
There's	red one.

What was there on the tray? Can you remember?

There was	some coins.
	a book.
There were	a glass of water.

Asking questions:

Is there	a watch on the tray?
Was there	a credit card?
Are there	any books on the table?
Were there	any bananas?

Put some things on the table. Look at the things for one minute. Then stop looking and ask your partner questions like the ones above.

Now put the things away, and write three sentences about the things that *were* on the table.

a

How many aunts have I got?

A British family in Victorian days
Queen Victoria was born in 1819 and became Queen in 1837 at the age of 18. She married Prince Albert in 1840 and they had 9 children. She was Queen for 63 years until she died in 1901. There were a lot of large families in Victorian times.

JRW

b I have five brothers and sisters. Both my sisters live in London.
How many brothers have I got?

c Both my friend's sons go to school, but neither of his daughters does.
How many children does he have?

d Two of Bob's sisters and both his brothers live in England. His other sister lives in America.
How many children do Bob's parents have?

e Both June's younger brothers play tennis, but neither of her older brothers does. All her sisters like tennis. She has more brothers than sisters.
How many brothers and sisters does she have?

Can you explain the answers to the class? Say things like this.

'Both' means there are two. 'All' means more than two.

f Charles is good at languages. He has a lot of books. They are in different languages, and they are different colours – red, blue and yellow.

1 Both the large yellow books are English dictionaries.
2 Neither of the small yellow books is in English.
3 There are more yellow books than small blue books.
4 All the small blue books are in French.
5 Both the large blue books are in German.
6 There are fifteen books altogether.

How many books are there of each colour?

---

47 Offering things to people

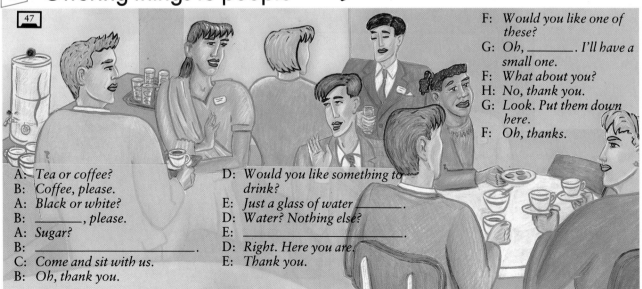

A: *Tea or coffee?*
B: *Coffee, please.*
A: *Black or white?*
B: *_____, please.*
A: *Sugar?*
B: *_____.*
C: *Come and sit with us.*
B: *Oh, thank you.*

D: *Would you like something to drink?*
E: *Just a glass of water _____.*
D: *Water? Nothing else?*
E: *_____.*
D: *Right. Here you are.*
E: *Thank you.*

F: *Would you like one of these?*
G: *Oh, _____. I'll have a small one.*
F: *What about you?*
H: *No, thank you.*
G: *Look. Put them down here.*
F: *Oh, thanks.*

a Question words

You have seen these question words in Units 1–3:

How ...?

What ...? When ...? Where ...?
Which ...? Who ...? Why ...?

Can you remember which words complete these sentences?

1. _____'s that? _____'s his surname?
2. _____'s your address?
3. _____ are these people?
4. _____'s David from?
5. _____ do you spell that?
6. _____ number is missing – 1 2 3 5 6 ?
7. _____ are your parents called?
8. _____ about your father?
9. _____ many children have you got?
10. _____ much can you remember?
11. _____ does 'sort of' mean?
12. _____ is the key word in each phrase?
13. _____ does Bridget say 'reddish' not 'red'?
14. _____ do words in English end in 's'?
15. _____ do we say 'is' and when do we say 'are'?

b Things people say

Would you like tea or coffee?
Tea, please.
Would you like one of these?
Yes please.
No thank you.

Would you close the door please.
Would you put the light on/off.
Can you hold this please?
Could you carry this for me?
– Yes, of course!

c One, two or more?

there are two white shapes
both the white shapes
neither of the white shapes
both of them
neither of them

there are some yellow shapes
there are three yellow shapes
all of the yellow ones
none of the yellow ones
some of them
all of them
none of them

one of them
this one
the first one
the second one
the third one
mine
yours

d Where?

in the middle
next to
between
on the left/right
to the left/right of
above
below

e him, her, them

Do you know	him her	
Come and meet	them	? .

Make sentences about some of the people in the list.

That's Mrs Kent. Do you know her?

Mrs Kent   Miss Green
David Foll   Jenny
Charles and his wife Danny
those people

f Which person?

... the man with blonde hair ...
... the woman wearing a grey skirt ...
The man is carrying a brown bag.
His hair is brown.
She's got fair hair.

g you, me, us

Come and sit with	us. me.
Can I sit with	you?

h Find the odd word out

In 1, **ruler** is the odd word out. You can wear all the other things, but you can't wear a ruler!
Find the odd word out in each of the other groups.

1. shirt, ruler, watch, trousers, blouse, glasses
2. first, second, third, four
3. more, bigger, same, smaller, older, younger
4. above, below, to the left, on the right, with a hat, in the middle
5. black, white, red, large, green, blue
6. hair, arm, hand, head, heart, hat, eyes

Important words to remember (229 so far)

age	carry	glass	left	second	was
all	clothes	green	light	shape	water
another	coffee	grey	middle	shoe	wear
arm	colour	group	mine	show	were
bag	course	hair	neither	some	white
because	dark	hand	next	sort	why
become	difference	hat	none	square	with
between	eye	head	nothing	tea	would
black	face	him	ones	them	yellow
blue	foot	hold	part	there	yours
body	forget	lady	pink	these	
brown	French	language	red	third	
car	game	large	repeat	us	

Unit 4
A house or a flat?

Buildings

Look at these buildings. Find:

    a block of flats (an apartment block)
    a detached house
    a semi-detached house
    a terraced house
    an office block
    a bungalow
    a country cottage

Read these definitions.

detached house one not joined to another house
semi-detached house one joined to the house next door by a shared wall
room separate part of a house/building with its own walls, ceiling and floor and door
flat set of rooms for living in, usually on one floor
block large building (block of flats, office block)
terraced house one of a row of similar houses joined together by their side walls
bungalow house with only one storey
cottage small house usually in the country

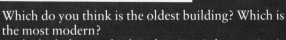

Which do you think is the oldest building? Which is the most modern?
And which do you think is the nicest? the prettiest? the most expensive? the easiest to live in?

23

50 Homes

50a **a** Charles and Bob both live in Birmingham. Bob lives in a part of Birmingham called West Heath. Charles lives in Edgbaston.

Bob asks Charles if he lives in a house or a flat. What does Charles say?
Then Charles asks Bob. What does Bob say?

b What sort of house or flat do you live in?

Is it big or small? . . . quite big? . . . very big?
An old house or a modern house?

▷ Find out about your partner's home and tell the class. ◁

Charles and Bob

51 Rooms

Which room are these people in?
Are they in the bedroom, the bathroom, the kitchen, the dining-room or the sitting-room (living-room)?

Which room do you think is the nicest? Why?

Close your books and see how much you can remember. Ask each other questions.

▷ Close your books again and write one sentence about each person or group of people. Read your sentences. Your partner will look at the pictures and tell you if they are true or not. ◁

52 David and Bridget's homes

52a **a** David asks Bridget where she lives. Say if these sentences are *true* or *not true*.

1 *Bridget lives in a big flat.*   4 *It's her own flat.*
2 *It has two bedrooms.*   5 *It's not an old flat.*
3 *It has a small dining-room.*

52b **b** Bridget asks David where he lives. Look at the plan of his flat. Can you say which rooms are which?

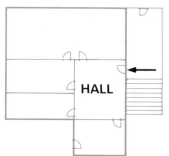

HALL

53 *Language study* . . . .

a **or**
50a Are there any questions with **or**? How many? Write them down and learn them.

Can you remember what questions Bob and Charles asked about each other's homes? These are their answers.

CO: I live in a house, in Edgbaston.
CO: It's a semi-detached house.
BB: Erm . . . nineteen thirties . . .

Listen again and check.

b **quite, sort of, very**
52a Listen to Bridget telling David about her flat again and find Bridget's exact answers to these questions.

Is her flat small?
Is it modern?

This is what Bridget says about her flatmate.

BG: We're both different. We've both got different friends, so it works out well because we both lead our own lives and yet we get on well when we're – we are in the flat together.

53b Listen very carefully. We have left some words out of the transcript. What words? What do they mean?

54 | What kind of home?

Bridget lives in a small top floor flat. It is quite modern and has two bedrooms, a sitting-room, a kitchen and a bathroom. She shares it with her flatmate.

Find a new partner and find out about their house or flat.

▶ Write about it.
Also write about your own flat or house. ◀

Let your partner read what you have written. Did you say the same things?

55 | The largest... the smallest... the most expensive...

Bridget's flat has five rooms. Most family houses in Britain have two or three bedrooms, a bathroom, kitchen, sitting-room and dining-room – about six or seven rooms altogether. Prices vary.

A small family house about 20 miles from London cost about £70,000 in 1987. In other parts of Britain the same kind of house would be much less, perhaps as little as £20,000. But in London, the same house could be £150,000.   JDW

a How many rooms do most family houses have in your own country?
How much do small family houses cost?

b Read about the houses below. Which one is:

the most expensive house in the world?
the largest private house in the world?
the smallest house in Britain?

_____ is Biltmore House in Asheville, North Carolina, USA, belonging to the Vanderbilt family. It was built in 1890 at a cost of US$4,100,000. It has 250 rooms and stands in an estate of 48,100 hectares.

_____ is the Hearst Ranch at San Simeon, California. It was built for the newspaper owner, William Randolph Hearst in 1922–39 at a cost of US$30,000,000. It has over 100 rooms and a garage for 25 cars.

_____ is a cottage in North Wales built in the nineteenth century. It is 10 feet (309 cms) high, and measures only 6 feet (182 cms) across the front. It has a tiny staircase and two tiny rooms.

▶ **c** Look at the photographs. Write one or two more sentences about each of the houses. Begin: 'It ...' Check your sentences carefully. ◀

Give your sentences to other students to read. Can they say which house each sentence is about?

56 | *Grammar words*

in

Can you find six phrases with the word **in** in the texts about the houses in section 55 above? When is **in** used with time, and when with place?

How many of these examples are about place? What about the others?

In fact there are more men in your family.
Bridget lives in a small top floor flat in London.
Which room are these people in?
Good morning, please come in!
The largest private house in the world is in Asheville.
It was built in 1890.
Do you know the names of the letters in English?

57 | The old flat

a David lives by himself in a ground-floor flat. It's quite small but it's near the shops and it's got a small garden.

Bridget asked him about his flat, then she asked him:

BG: Where did you live before you lived in your flat now?

57a Which flat do you think David likes best, and why?

b Bridget had to move out of her old flat because the owner came back from America and wanted to live there again. David asked Bridget which of the two flats she liked better – her old one, or the one she lives in now.

57b Which flat did Bridget like better? Why?

25

58 Becky's homes

The authors' teenage daughter, Becky, wrote this.

We live in a four-bedroom semi-detached house in a town called Hemel Hempstead, about twenty miles from London. It was built in about 1960.

When we lived in Birmingham, from 1979 to 1981, we lived in an old house in a district called Harborne. It was a large semi-detached house built in the 1890s with five bedrooms and nice big rooms downstairs. It had a big garden at the back but no front garden. It was a really nice house, much nicer than our house in Hemel Hempstead. **BW**

Look at the two pictures. Which house is which? How do you know?

59 *Language study*

do and **did** with **live**

Find three phrases with **live** or **lived** in the text in section 58. What is the difference in meaning between **live** and **lived**?

59 Which of these sentences are about the past and which are about the present?

Where do you live?
I live in a house in Edgbaston.
Where did you live before?
I lived in the next street.
Why did you move?

Practise some questions from the tables with your partner.

Where	do did	*you live?* *they live?* *Charles and his wife live?* *your friends live?*

Where	does did	*he live?* *she live?* *Bridget live?* *your friend live?*

60 Your home

Where do you live now?
Where did you live before?

Where did you live as a child? What was it like?

Which was the best place to live? Why?

Talk to your partner. Compare places you have lived in.

▶ Tell the class about where you lived as a child. Prepare carefully. ◀

Listen to the others talking and find out how many people lived in the same kind of home as you did.

▶ Write either about where you lived, or about where your partner lived as a child. ◀

61 *Classroom language*

61

S: *What's the difference between 'did' and 'do'?*
T: *Well, 'did' is used to talk about the past ... and 'do' (and 'does') are for things that still happen sometimes ...*

S: *I'm sorry, I didn't bring my book.*
T: *Never mind! Can you share with someone?*
S: *Yes, fine.*

62 *English sounds*

62 What sounds do the words in each of these sets have in common?

1 live, very, five, expensive, seven, have, evening

2 big, Bridget, black, Bob, number, about, because

Grammar words

a a, an

We use **a** or **an** when we are talking about something which is not the only one.

Bridget lives in a small top floor flat ... (there are a lot of small top floor flats)

Have you got a phone number?

A or **an** is also used in expressions of quantity (**a lot, a lot of, a few, a bit**); and to mean one only.

Look at **a** and **an** in the Grammar Book.

b it

What does **it** mean in each example?

David lives by himself in a ground-floor flat. It's quite small but it's near the shops.

Have you got a phone number?
Yes it's two six two.

What is the difference between **it**, **he** (**him**) and **she** (**her**)?

c the

Do you know the names ...
Which names?
Do you know the names of the students in your class?

Biltmore House is the ... *house* ...
Which house?
Biltmore House is the biggest house in the world.

The lady ... *is blonde.*
Which lady?
The lady in my picture is blonde.

Look at these uses of the **the** and answer the question 'Which one?'.

JV: And the man in the middle of the picture has blue trousers.
DL: So has mine.
JV: The woman next to him has orange trousers. [...]
DL: What colour shoes has the lady on the far left got in your picture?
JV: She's got brown shoes.
DL: Ah, mine has red.
JV: The man has black shoes.

d So when we are talking about one of many, and we do not know which one, we say **a** or **an**. When we know which one, we say **it** or **the**.

Wordpower

nice
What could these people be saying?

Do you like it?
Yes, it's nice.

Do you like living there?
Is it a nice flat?

Was it nice, that place?

It wasn't as nice as the flat I've got now.

It was a really nice house, much nicer than the house we live in now. It had nice big rooms downstairs.

Nice day isn't it?
Hello. Nice to meet you.
Goodbye. Nice meeting you.
He's nice, isn't he?
Thanks, that's really nice of you.

If we like something we say 'It's nice'.
What do you say in your language?

Asking permission

65
A: *Mrs French, may I borrow this for a moment please?*
B: *The newspaper? Yes, fine.*
A: *Thank you.*

C: *Would you mind if we had the TV on?*
B: *No, that's fine, but not too loud!*
C: *All right.*

D: *Do you mind if I smoke?*
E: *No, not really. I'll get an ashtray.*
B: *But not while we're eating, okay?*
D: *Oh, no, of course not!*

E: *Could we have the window open please?*
B: *Yes, if that's all right with you others?*
E: *Yeah, sure.*

a biggest, most, best ...

The largest house in the world belongs to the Vanderbilt family. Biltmore House is the biggest house in the world, but the Hearst Ranch is the most expensive.
The smallest house in Britain is only ten feet high.
'Nice' is one of the commonest words in English.

Look at how these words are formed.

nicer	nicest
bigger	biggest
prettier	prettiest
more expensive	most expensive
commoner/ more common	commonest/ most common
better	best

Are you good at names? You're better than me! But Bridget had the best memory – much better than us ...

Which room was the nicest?
Which did you like the best?

b ????

The same word is missing from each of these sentences. What word?

Mmm. Very good. Much better memory _____ me.
Your family has more women and girls _____ men and boys.
There are more yellow books _____ small blue books.
It was much nicer _____ the flat I've got now.

66b Can you hear the missing word?

c What was it like?

very good, really nice, quite big, sort of modern

David's old flat was quite nice.
It was quite a nice flat.
His new flat is very nice.
Our house in Harborne was quite big.
It was really nice.
It was a really nice house.
The Vanderbilts' house is very very big.
Our new house is sort of modern.

d Where in the world?

What's the difference?

Jenny lives in North London.
Birmingham is north of London.

Look at a map of the British Isles and find a big town in each of these places:

in the	north	of	England
	south		Scotland
	west		Wales
	east		Ireland

Say things about places you know, like this.

I live			3		south		here.
_____	is	about	5	miles	east	of	_____
_____			20	kms	north		_____
_____			30		west		

e own

1 belonging to

What words come before **own**?

room   separate part of a house
... with its own walls, ceiling and floor.
It's my first flat.
BG: *Ah, right, and it's your own.* DF: *Yeah.*
We both lead our own lives and yet we get on well together.
It's not her own flat.
Do you have rooms like any of these in your own home?
... in your own country ...

2 alone, not together with someone else

Do it on your own, by yourself.
He lives on his own.
I live on my own.

f less ..., not so ...

less common
less expensive
not so expensive
not so pretty
not so big
not so nice
not so good

	expensive pretty big nice good small	
not as		as the other o

Important words to remember (292 so far)

a	common	furniture	mind	pound	the	
alone	cost	garden	modern	question	together	
an	did	hall	most	quite	very	
answer	do	home	move	really	wall	
back	door	house	much	room	west	
bed	east	in	new	share	window	
borrow	expensive	its	north	sit	world	
bring	fine	kitchen	now	south	yet	
building	flat	less	open	stairs		
chair	floor	live	out	table		
close	front	may	own	than		

Unit 5
Revision Unit

67　A street scene

This street is called Montague Street Precinct. It's a shopping street in Worthing, a small town in Sussex, on the south coast of England.

Are these sentences *true* or *not true*?

a　*There's a fish and chip shop on the left hand side of the street.*
b　*The fish and chip shop is between Radio Rentals and the newsagents.*
c　*The shop to the left of the newsagents is to let.*
d　*There's a menswear shop more or less opposite the newsagents.*
e　*Some of the shops are clothes shops.*
f　*None of these shops are supermarkets.*
g　*One of the shops on the left sells food.*
h　*All the shops are quite small and very modern.*
i　*There are two girls walking together, both wearing white tops.*

j　*Both the girls are eating ice-creams.*
k　*Neither of the girls has got a handbag.*
l　*All the people in the street are girls or women.*
m　*Most of the people in the street are girls and women.*
n　*There are more men than women shopping here.*
o　*There's a man wearing a blue suit on the right, behind the two girls.*
p　*His wife's hair is red.*

> Write five sentences of your own about the picture. Make some true, and some not true. Read them out to the class. The other students must say 'true' or 'not true' without looking at the picture again.

68　*Wordpower*

like

Look at these examples with your partner, and answer the questions.

1　meaning the same as or similar to

Have you got any clothes like the clothes in the picture?

Are the shops in your country like the ones in Montague Street?

Are the girls in the picture secretaries, students or teachers?

I think they look like _____

2　used when giving examples

A newsagent sells newspapers, magazines and things like ice-cream and cigarettes. Do newsagents do the same in your country?

Words like 'baby', 'university', which end in 'y', change to 'babies', 'universities' when you add an 's'. What about the word 'family'?

3　used when talking about things that you think are nice
4　used when talking about things that you want.

Read these three dialogues with a friend. Find the phrases with **like**. Which meaning does each **like** have – 3 or 4?

A:　Can I help you?
B:　Yes, I'd like two ice-creams please. Two of those.
A:　Would you like chocolate or vanilla?
B:　Vanilla. (to a friend) I don't like chocolate ice-cream. Do you?

A:　I like Worthing. I'd like to come back here.
B:　Yes it's nice. I like it as well.

A:　Shall we go and have a drink?
B:　Yes, I'd like to. I need a drink after that ice-cream.
A:　So do I.

69 Song

Is this a sad song
or a happy one?

Portland town

I was born in Portland town,
I was born in Portland town,
Yes I was, yes I was,
Yes, I was.

I was born in Portland town,
Got married in Portland town,
Yes I did, yes I did,
Yes, I did.

Got married in Portland town,
Had children, one, two, three,
Yes I did, yes I did,
Yes, I did.

They sent them away to war,
Ain't got no kids[1] no more,
No I ain't, no I ain't,[2]
No, I ain't.

[1] kids = children
[2] Ain't means 'haven't'.
    ain't got no = haven't got any

70 Picture puzzle

Look carefully at the two pictures here. Can you find
seven things that are different? Write down the
differences quickly, in note form. For example:

> 7 differences
> A – cat on R. of sign.
> B – cat on L.

▶ Then help each other to write sentences. ◀

A

B

70 Did Bridget and David find the same things as you
did? Write down any differences that you didn't find
before.

What was the second difference Bridget and David
found? (What words tell you that it wasn't the first
difference?)
Now, can you find out which was the first difference
Bridget and David found? Are you sure?

▶ Each group read out a sentence about one
difference.
Together, make a list of all the differences.

71 Your family

This is Hideo Ogimura.
He works in a bank in
Kyoto. He goes to
English lessons three
days a week.

This is what Hideo wrote
about a member of his family.

My ....., Mrs Chiyo Ogimura was born in Tokyo.
She now lives in Kobe near Tokyo. She is married
and has two sons aged 12 and 14, and a daughter
aged 9. She works in a bookshop. Her husband
is an engineer.

Who do you think Mrs Chiyo Ogimura is? Is she
Hideo's mother? His mother's sister? His wife? His
sister? His brother's wife?

Write a short paragraph about a member of
your family. Do not write who it is.

Where were they born? How old are they?
What family do they have? Where do they live?
What work do they do?

Read your paragraph to the people in your
group. Can they guess what member of your
family it is about?

72 Find the differences

AT THE ESTATE AGENT

a Group A look at the picture on page 99.
Group B look at the picture on page 100.

Each student from
group A find a student
from group B. Talk
about your pictures but
don't show them to
each other. Find the
differences.

▶ How many differences did you find?
Tell the class about them.

Are there any differences you didn't find? Check the
number of differences you now have.

72b b David and Bridget tried to find seven
differences. Which seven did they find?

Language study

a Read transcript 70, and find the following:

1 fifteen questions

Do any of the questions have the same words or phrases in them? Put the questions in groups (for example, put all the questions with the word **shall** together) and write them all down.

2 five phrases with **and** and four phrases with **but**

Read these to your partner.

3 seven examples of **Yes** or **Yeah**

Write down the words that come after them (for example, *Yes, it is*).

4 five examples of the word **so**

Where does **so** come in most sentences?

b Useful idioms

Match a phrase from the left with a phrase from the right that means the same thing.

Doesn't matter.	*Wait a minute.*
Anything else?	*Never mind.*
Hang on.	*Any other things?*

BG: Oh. Do you think –?
DF: Doesn't matter. Thirty in picture A and thirteen . . .
BG: Thirteen in picture B. And this number's different.
DF: What number?
BG: The phone number of Paul Smith and Sons.
DF: Oh yeah. So, the phone number of Paul

Stories

Read the three stories and try to guess what the last words are.

a

I was sitting in the kitchen listening to a local radio station when I heard the disc jockey announce, 'This next record is for Pat Malone, who is a hundred and eleven.'
There was a pause, then, 'My goodness, that *is* old, isn't it!'
Another pause. 'Oh, I'm sorry, I got that wrong. This record is for Pat Malone, who . . .

– is in bed.   – is ill.   – is 11.   – is 101.

1   Find all the examples of **was** and **is**. Which words come before and after them? Read the phrases to your partner. When is it **was** and not **is**?

2   What words do you say for **My goodness!** in your language?

b

A psychiatrist, receiving a new patient, saw that she was carrying a duck under her arm. Saying nothing about the duck, he asked her to sit down.
'Well,' he said, 'can I help you?'
'Oh, it's not me who needs help, doctor,' she replied, 'it's my husband here. He thinks . . .

Past and present forms

Match the verbs.

asked	said	is	has
went	was	see	hear
saw	heard	go	ask
thought	had	say	think

c

– Oh, no, darling! Not again! I think you should go and see a psychiatrist . . ., please dear!
– Oh, all right, then.

A man dressed as Napoleon went to see a psychiatrist at the urging of his wife.
'What's your problem?' asked the doctor.
'I have no problem,' replied the man. 'I'm one of the most famous people in the world. I have a great army behind me, I have all the money I'll ever need, and I live in great luxury.'
'Then why are you here?'
'It's my wife,' said the man. 'She thinks . . .

What is the problem, do you think? What did he say to the psychiatrist? Tell each other what you think he said.

Find these words in the story. Which is the odd one out? Why?

asked, dressed, replied, said

Language study

Short questions

72b   Which sentences below need a question mark, and which a full stop?

DF: Two fourteen
BG: Yes And you – . . . Yes
DF: Is it Okay Mine's _____ , High Street I've got a _____ underneath that Have you
BG: No, I haven't
DF: How many have we got to get Seven
DF: And there seems to be a child, is that Behind the chair
BG: No

Find some more short questions in transcript 72b. What do they mean?

Key (74)

– is ill.   – he's a duck.   – she's Mrs Smith.

a said, say, says, saying

People *say* things in English. Books, newspapers and signs *say* things. It *says* things in brochures, on T-shirts and on notices. How do you say **say** in your language?

A: *Sorry, what did you say?*
B: *I said, 'See you Friday'.*
They said thank you and went home.
He says his meeting starts at seven.
I don't know what to say.

There's a sign outside saying 'Open all day Sunday'.
She wrote and said she's going to Spain.

What does it say on your T-shirt?
It said on the radio it's going to rain.

Excuse me, how do you say this in English?

Note the pronunciation: **said** = /sed/, **says** = /sez/, but **say** = /sei/.

b these, those

A: *I'd like some of those, please.* B: *Some of these?* A: *Yes, please.*
A: *Look at that car!* B: *And those boys on bicycles...*
Look at this picture and read these sentences.
Say these phrases to your partner.

c ever

I have all the money I'll ever need.
Do you ever carry a bag like the girl on the right?
Do you ever write your name like this?
Have you ever eaten British fish and chips?

d well

How do you say **well** in your language? Do you have the same word for all these meanings?

1 at or near the start of a sentence, when you are speaking and don't know what to say
Well... shall we start?
Okay, well, ... well, what have we got...?
Well, I'm not sure...
BG: *... she's got red boots.*
DF: *Well – these look sort of brown.*

2 meaning 'good', but used with a verb
Mr Johnson? I don't know him very well.
I can't speak French very well, but my Spanish is quite good.
Paul Young was quite a well known singer in 1985.
Well done! Very good!

3 as well, as well as
BG: *I've got [...] a telephone.*
[...] DF: *Yes, I've got that as well.*
A: *My name's Richard.* B: *Oh, my name's Richard as well!*
The woman outside the Estate Agents has got a large bag as well as a handbag.

e inside, outside

... two people sitting at a desk inside.
... a bicycle parked outside.
The car's outside the Post Office.

Ask your partner: *What is there outside your classroom/home?*

f need

I need a drink.
I have all the money I'll ever need.
How much money do you need?

g this, that

Excuse me, is this Mr Johnson's office?
June, this is Mrs Kent...
A: *Is this yours?* B: *Oh, yes, that's mine. Thank you very much.*
A: *Excuse me, is this right?* B: *That's correct, yes.*
Write it like this, look.
Hello. This is Jane here. Who's that speaking please?
This is London. BBC World Service. The time is...
That's the end of News about Britain. The time is...
A: *That was a nice lesson, thank you.* B: *Oh, that's all right.*
A: *That's it!* B: *Yes, that's it, we've finished, good.*

this lesson   this evening
this week   this Friday

h side

DF: *Where is it?* BG: *Erm... on the left hand side.*
BG: *... two people sitting at a desk inside.* DF: *What, one on each side of the desk?*
There are shops on both sides of Montague Street.
It's not on this side of the road... it's on the other side.

i on

Is that your book on the table?
Are you coming to class on Monday?
Worthing is a small town on the south coast.

Can you find eleven other examples of the word **on** on this page? Write them down.

address am and are ask book can class come day different eight either eleven English example first five form four Friday friend from goodbye he hello her his I is know learn letter London look me meet Miss Monday Mr Mrs my name nice nine no not number of one or page people person phone photograph please read same Saturday say secretary seven she six student Sunday surname teacher tell ten this three Thursday today tomorrow tonight true Tuesday twelve two use Wednesday what where who word write yes you your about any baby big both boy brother but call carefully child daughter family father find finish get girl had have how husband it key list listen lot man many married mean money more mother office okay old our parent picture plan remember right shall sister small so son sorry start stop talk thank their they thing useful we which wife woman yeah young age all another arm bag because become between black blue body brown car carry clothes coffee colour course dark difference eye face foot forget French game glass green grey group hair hand hat head ... at second shape shoe show some sort square tea the ... er back bed borrow bring building chair close com... ... kitchen less live may mind modern most move muc... ... he together very wall west window world yet army ... on opposite outside paper paragraph problem radi... ... r well after afternoon ago almost American April A... ...each easy England evening exact examination excep... ...on January July June just last level make March M... ... personal probably quarter ring September sir soun... ...lso bad better bit buy cent cheap enjoy fashionable ... ...er price report short size society someone sport st... ...ge dinner during early else every everythin... ...times supper tend then till university usually vary v... ...wn education end entrance exactly fact far further hospital into map mile near park pass past place police primary road school station straight street system through traffic turn until up walk enough few herself himself instead itself myself play round themselves try used without yourself yourselves business busy country drive government important labour law lie life meeting parliament particularly party political politician present press recently rest seem sleep social spend stay such travel trip village visit wrong Africa alive always America as autumn bell bottom Britain British century coast cold dead decide degree detail Europe even experience farm forest France happen here high hill history hot idea later let mountain never perhaps possible pretty put rain reason river roof run Scotland sea season single sky spring state summer sun suppose top type weather will winter above again arrange arrive been below future lose receive should soon therefore understand whether available daily emergency especially fire free hear help if instruction keep machine necessary power private public service situation speak telephone whatever while within air chance figure holiday hope however love miss set since towards

Important words to remember (334 so far)

army	famous	need	paper	shopping	television
born	food	news	paragraph	side	that
desk	go	newspaper	problem	sign	those
doctor	great	off	radio	something	town
drink	ill	on	reply	song	tree
eat	inside	opposite	send	stand	war
ever	like	outside	shop	story	well

Unit 6
Just over eight million

bank account number

N93 Night Bus

The South West (A30...)
Central London (A4)
Guildford (A3)
Portsmouth

Hammersmith Bridge 1⁄2
Chiswick 11⁄2
Putney Bridge 13⁄4

flat · raffle ticket · house

top of the pops

flight

tennis score

football score

car number

77 Numbers

a We use numbers for a lot of different things.

Can you find a telephone number?
Can you find the number of a house?
What other numbers are there?

floor

Elspeth Lang
7 Potter Lane
London SW13

for money

emergency number

Open Monday to Friday
Lunchtimes 12.30pm-3pm
Evenings 6.30pm-3am
Now open Saturdays 8pm-3am
Fully Air Conditioned

ESHER. Attractive Victorian semi, four
bedrooms, two bathrooms. £149,000.

You are invited to a
PICNIC
In Green Park
at 12pm
on July 30th 198...

WIMBLEDON Tkts. Buy/sell.
Pop Shows. 247 6036, 377 5500.
WIMBLEDON tkts wanted. All
days. All tkts. 930 1566.

...5143/4294

block

closing time

FLIGHT BA0662 /29 DATE DEST SVG CLASS M SERVICE INFORMATION

NAME DURY A SEAT NR 21A

1ST · CLUB · ECON · ECON 21A

road sign

seat number

telephone

post code

BBC World Service

Lloyds Bank Plc

dialling code

A961 GPL

Wednesday NOVEMBER 6 13 20 27

time

2300 World News
09 Commentary
15 Good Books
30 Top Twenty

cash card

bus

price

"778485" 30"9374" 0202596"

bus stand

Mon - Fri
Midnight - 7am
9pm - Midnight

Sat
Midnight - 7am
1pm - Midnight

Sun
At any time

Except
permit holders

weight

date

opening hours

parking notice

THE THREE CHURCHES P.C.C. № 1706

Grand Summer Fete Draw

FIRST PRIZE £100
Twenty Other Prizes

20p TICKET: TWENTY PENCE 20p

999 emergencies

Fire · Police · Amb...
Cave Rescue · Coastguard · Mountain...

platform

73 Islington Kings Cross
Euston Oxford Street
Knightsbridge Kensington
HAMMERSMITH BDY

29 481 365
EXPIRES END 01/87

VOID VOID VOID

TO LONDON LHR AZ 0279 Y VOID VOID ON...
TO ROME FCO AZ 0174 Y 16OCT 2025 ON...
TO VENICE VCE OPEN 18OCT 2045 ON...
TO LONDON LHR C
FARE 384.00 16OCT86LON AZ ROM 171.00YB AZ VCE YY LON 213.00

b All these announcements and messages have numbers in them. Where might you hear them, and what are the numbers?

c What numbers do you keep in your head? Can you remember, for example:

your best friend's birthday?
your own birthday?
your telephone number?
your best friend's telephone number?
your passport number?

In *one minute* write down all the numbers you can remember. Say the numbers you have written down, and ask your partner to guess what they are.

Tell the class what they were. How many different things did you remember numbers for?

Sorry. wrong number.

33

78 Ways of saying numbers

78a **a** How do you say telephone numbers in your language?

b Look at the numbers on the right. What are they?

What about 1989 for example? Could it be a telephone number, or a date, or a car number? How would you say it if it was a date? One thousand nine hundred and eighty-nine? ... One nine eight nine ...?

Discuss with your partner how you could say the numbers. How many different ways can you find and what do they each mean?

▶ Tell the class. ◀

22

0

1989

3.14

748

22756 **10.12**

021 3370452

78c **c** Bridget and David talked about the same numbers.
Did they think of the same things as you? Write down the things David and Bridget thought of.

79 *Language study*

Possibility

a BG: Yeah. Seven four eight for a plane number, or seven hundred and fort-– well – no.
DF: Your house number could be seven hundred and forty-eight but a bus would be seven four eight as well.
BG: Yes. . . . Yes. Er, ten twelve. That could be the time. You'd just say ten twelve. The date you'd say –
DF: Mhm. . . . Or twelve minutes past ten.
BG: either the tenth of December or the twelfth of October
DF: Mhm.
BG: depending on whether it was English or American.

1 Why does David say:

DF: Your house number could be seven hundred and forty-eight . . .

2 What does Bridget say about **ten twelve**?

3 What do you think **'d** means?

79b **b** *What if it was a bus?*
You'd say twenty-two.
If it was a bus you'd say twenty-two.
You'd say twenty-two if it was a bus.

c If you were counting, how would you say these numbers?

30 33 300 313 330 3,313

How about these?

55 15 5,950 4,995 50 5,250,000 500

79c Which number comes first? Which is second? Which number is missing each time?

Now you do the same with your partner. Read the numbers and miss one out.

80 Wordpower

about, nearly, something, over, under, almost

a We don't usually say numbers like four thousand eight hundred and ninety-six. Usually we would say 'About five thousand' or 'Nearly five thousand'.

Can you match the numbers to the right words?

5,123	Five thousand and something
308	under three hundred
2,573	about two and a half thousand
4,876	nearly five thousand
2,435	just under two thousand five hundred
11,436	three hundred and something
2,400	over ten thousand
289	just over five thousand
	almost five thousand

But sometimes we have to be exact!

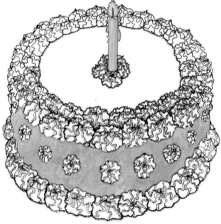

– *What's your phone number?*
– *Just over eight million.*

b Write down any number under 100. Do not tell it to your partner.

Guess what your partner's number is, by asking 'Is it under 50?', 'Is it over 20?' etc. Your partner can only answer 'yes' or 'no'.

81 When's your birthday?

81a **a** Bridget, Jenny, David and Danny tried to find out if they or any of their close relatives had birthdays on the same day.

Make a note of their birthdays.
Do any of them have birthdays on the same day? Which are closest?
Do any of you have birthdays on one of the days they said?

b Make a list of four different people's birthdays: your own birthday and the birthdays of three close friends or relatives. Talk to the other students in your group. Can you find two people with birthdays on the same day?

a Mr Marconi has one daughter, Elsa, who wants to go to England to improve her spoken English. He saw an advert for English courses at the Regent School of English in London, so he wrote them a letter. Read his letter and find out what kind of classes Elsa wants.

b Write a letter to enquire about a school for yourself in Oxford. Say that:

– you have heard about the school from a friend.
– you are an elementary student.
– you are taking an examination in six months' time.
– you would like a month's lessons.

Say when you would like to go. Ask the school for the information you need.

c This is some of the information about conversation classes and individual tuition from the brochure that the school sent to Mr Marconi. Find out which course(s) would be best for Elsa and how much it will cost altogether for one month.

Via S. Eufemia 5,
00187 Roma,

Tel: 456 1239

3/1/85

The Director
Regent School of English
19/23 Oxford Street
London
W1R 1RF

Dear Sir

I saw an advertisement for your school at the British Council Centre this week.

I would like my daughter, Elsa, aged 17, to study English in London for about a month in April this year. She needs to improve her Spoken English so I would like to enrol her for a conversation course. It would be very good if she could also have an hour's individual tuition every day.

I would be grateful if you could send me your brochure and enrolment forms for this year's courses.

I look forward to hearing from you.

Yours sincerely

Mario Marconi

Mario Marconi

SPECIAL COURSES

Conversation Courses†

Levels: Intermediate to Advanced
Length of Course: 4 weeks
Courses start on a Tuesday
Daily programme 12.05 – 12.55 Mon – Fri (Total 18 lessons)

Ref.	Starting date:
OC1	3 FEB
OC2*	14 APR
OC3	1 SEP
OC4	29 SEP
Tuition Fee: £40	

EASTER COURSE

Levels:	All levels except Beginners
Length of course:	2 weeks (9 days)
Daily programme:	09.00 – 12.00 and 13.00 – 15.00 (Total: 45 lessons)
Ref. & Dates	OEC1* 1 APR – 11 APR
Tuition Fee:	**£175**

NOTES REGENT SCHOOL LONDON	† signifies that these courses only take place if there is sufficient demand * signifies that a National Holiday falls within this course

INDIVIDUAL TUITION

General English — all levels accepted.
Times by arrangement with the Director of Studies.
Subject to availability.
Tuition Fee: £18 per 55-minute lesson

d This was the enrolment form the school sent. How do you think Elsa filled it in?

REGENT SCHOOLS OF ENGLISH
Enrolment Form

IMPORTANT:
TO BE COMPLETED IN FULL BY ALL STUDENTS AND SENT TOGETHER WITH YOUR DEPOSIT TO THE APPROPRIATE SCHOOL OR LOCAL REPRESENTATIVE (SEE ADDRESSES ON BACK PAGE)

Family name:

First name:

Nationality:

First language:

Age: Male/Female

Home address (in your own country):

Telephone:

How did you hear of the Regent School Organisation?

WHICH COURSE DO YOU WISH TO FOLLOW?

Please (✓) as appropriate

LONDON

GENERAL ENGLISH COURSES
☐ 5-lesson programme
☐ 3-lesson programme
☐ BUSINESS COMMUNICATION COURSE
☐ CONVERSATION COURSE
☐ EASTER COURSE
☐ CAMBRIDGE FIRST CERTIFICATE EXAM. COURSE
☐ CAMBRIDGE PROFICIENCY EXAM. COURSE
☐ ARELS HIGHER EXAMINATION COURSE

Course Reference(s):

Course dates:

from: to:

☐ INDIVIDUAL TUITION
    Number of lessons per day:

Course dates:

From: to:

83 *English sounds*

a Which sounds do the words in each set have in common?

1 British, English, ticket, fifty, big, pretty, women, business

2 green, jeans, sixteen, evening, leave, easy, between, kilo

b Now practise these phrases. First look at the phrase in brackets, and make sure you stress the right words.

It's easy to eat it. (not at all difficult)
Thirty kilos of big green apples? (or do you mean thirteen?)
Fifteen million people in the east of England... (not the west)

Now try changing the meaning by stressing other words in each example.

[84] The best time to phone

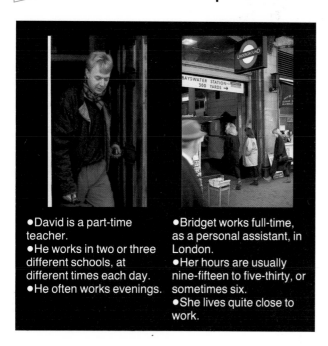

- David is a part-time teacher.
- He works in two or three different schools, at different times each day.
- He often works evenings.

- Bridget works full-time, as a personal assistant, in London.
- Her hours are usually nine-fifteen to five-thirty, or sometimes six.
- She lives quite close to work.

When is David usually in? What would be a good time to phone him? What about six o'clock in the evening?

What about Bridget? Could you phone her at home in the morning? What about six o'clock on Saturday morning?

[84] Look at the instructions David and Bridget had.

Make a note of the times and days they can phone each other.

```
Find out from your partner the best time to
phone them at home

- usually
- tomorrow
- next Saturday
- next Sunday

Don't write anything. When you've finished,
check that you have remembered correctly.
```

[85] *Language study*

Time phrases

[84] Write down each phrase which tells us:

1 about the time of day.   2 the day of the week.

e.g. *six o'clock in the evening*

[86] Phoning your partner

a Follow the instructions on the card in section 84.

▶ Get ready to tell the class when it is possible to phone your partner.

Who is the easiest person in the class to contact at home?
Who is the most difficult person to contact at home?

▶ **b** Write a message asking a friend to phone you in the next seven days. Give several different days and times for them to ring you, in case they are very busy.

Read other people's messages. Has anyone given the same times as you?

[87] *Classroom language*

[87]

S1: (thinks) *Oh no! Where's Angela? She's got my book.*
T: *Does anyone know where Angela is? Is she coming today?*
S2: *Well she rang last night and said she wasn't feeling well . . .*
S1: (thinks) *Oh dear . . . maybe she isn't coming . . .*

[88] *Grammar words*

it

1 pointing back
David lives in a ground floor flat. It's quite small, but it's near the shops.

2 pointing forward
It was nice to see you. [to see you was nice]

3 for time, weather etc.
In New York it's 8 a.m.
It's a nice day, isn't it?
It's my turn.
It works out very well, because we both lead our own lives.

4 for an unknown person
Who is it?

Which category do these examples belong to?

a *Read this and do what it says.*
b *It's easy to do it.*
c *Hello. Who is it?*
d *It's nice and warm today.*

[89] Telephoning

[89]

A: *Can I speak to Dr Brown please?*
B: *Certainly. Hold on, I'll put you through. . . . Sorry, I'm afraid she's out. She'll be back in about ten minutes. Can I take a message?*

90 Puzzle

What time is it in Rio de Janeiro?

a The time in London is 1 p.m. or 1300 hours. In New York, it's 8 a.m. or 0800 hours. It's 2200 hours in Tokyo, and 0500 in San Francisco. Write down what time it is in these places when it is the following times in England.

Cairo	2100 hours (9 p.m.)?
Berlin	0700 hours (7 a.m.)?
Rio de Janeiro	1500 hours (3 p.m.)?
Chicago	1000 hours (10 a.m.)?
Singapore	1400 hours (2 p.m.)?

90b **b** Do you agree with Danny and Jenny's times?

91 A telephone story

3 a.m. Wally is awakened by the phone ringing. He gets out of bed and goes downstairs – picks up the phone saying:
'Hello.'
'Hello. Is that Watford double two, double two?'
'No,' says Wally. 'This is Watford two two, two two.'
'Oh, I am sorry that you've been troubled.'

91 Now listen to the same joke again. Only this time it's a bit different because there is an extra last line.

92 Language study

think, thought

90b How many expressions can you hear with **think** or **thought**?

92 Practise these ways of agreeing and disagreeing.

I think so.	*I don't think so.*
I should think so.	*I wouldn't think so.*
I would think so.	*I wouldn't have thought so.*
I would have thought so.	

93 Grammar words

a **could, may, might, must, will**

90b Find the words **probably** and **definitely**. What is the difference in meaning?

93a Does the speaker sound a) *certain*, b) *not certain* or c) *very uncertain*? How do you know?

Make sentences from this table.

It may be John It could be John It might be John It must be John It'll be John	... .	*but I thought he was at work.* *It's possible, but I don't know.* *He's got dark hair.* *It can't be anyone else.* *He said 8.30.*

Read out your sentences. Read one that sounds *certain*, one that sounds *not certain* and one that sounds *very uncertain*.

b **for**

Do you have the same word for all these meanings of **for** in your language?

1 how long
David's been a teacher for 10 years.

1.1 when for
I've got four tickets for 10th August.

2 why
I went to Spain for a holiday.

2.1 **ask/look for**
We're looking for *a new house.*
I'll ask *them* for *help.*

3 who wants or needs ...
Please can you carry it for her?

3.1 after **good/bad, easy/difficult, right**
Is that all right for you?
It's difficult for me, *but never mind.*
Cigarettes are bad for your health.

Which categories do these examples go into?

a *I'm looking for David. Have you seen him anywhere?*
b *Hearst Ranch was built for William Randolph Hearst.*
c *I've got a lot of work for next week.*
d *Don't work too hard. It's not good for you.*
e *We use numbers for a lot of things.*
f *Sit down for a minute.*

Compare the sentences in each category with those in the Grammar Book.

Key (91)
'It's all right,' Wally replied, 'I had to come down as the phone was ringing.'

37

a way

There are different ways of writing 'colour' – the American way (color) or the English way (colour).
How many ways are there of saying this number?
Practise these ways of agreeing and disagreeing.
I like the way he sings.
Do it this way. Look.

b after, before

We use verbs like **lived, came** and **got** to talk about the past. What about the future? Look at the words in colour. Say whether they refer to the past, present or future.

after

I'll be in after ten o'clock tonight.
I'm going straight home after the lesson today.
After this, we'll do something else.
After a few minutes, he came back in.
I'll call you after I get home.
He lived in England for a few years, and after that he went to live in Spain.

before

I'll ring you before I go to work.
I always phone her before she goes out in the evening.
Don't call before nine in the morning.

c except

All levels except Beginners.
Ring me any day except Tuesday.
Any evening this week except tomorrow evening.

d ago

About 40 years ago, Jack lived in London.
I went to Africa twenty years ago.
A few months ago I met an old friend of mine.
I worked with her a long time ago – I can't remember what year.
They got married some time ago.

e time

How many words for **time** do you have in your language?

Can you tell me the time, please?
Do you have time to come round?
You know where I live, so come any time!
See you at the same time next week!
Next time you come, I'll give you the money.
In ten years' time, Birmingham will be very different.
He worked part-time to start with, then changed to full-time.

f this..., last..., next..., the other...

Past? Future? Either past or future?

Sort these phrases into three sets, for example:

last year (past)
next year (future)
this year (either)

this month
yesterday
last week
he came this month
tomorrow
next week
he's coming this month
this Sunday

tonight
the other day
last night
the other evening
He'll be here this week
tomorrow night
next Monday

g Can you wait?

Which of these examples is the odd one out? Why?

Just a moment ...
Half a moment ...
Just a minute ...
Wait a second ...
I won't be a second.
I'll be back in just a moment.
Sit down for a minute and I'll be with you.
Hang on a minute and I'll ask someone.
He paused for a moment.

h would

264? If it was a bus you would say two six four, but if you were counting, you'd say two hundred and sixty-four.

When would be a good time to phone you/to come and see you?

I would think so.
I would have thought so.

I'd like one of those please.
A: Would you like some tea? B: Yes please.
I would like to do another English course.

Important words to remember (420 so far)

after	could	fifty	just	nearly	thousand
afternoon	date	for	last	night	time
ago	December	forty	level	November	twenty
almost	definitely	forward	make	October	under
American	difficult	fourteen	March	over	wait
April	double	full	may	personal	way
August	each	general	May	probably	week
be	easy	half	might	quarter	weekend
before	England	hour	million	ring	when
best	evening	hundred	minute	September	year
birth	exact	individual	moment	sir	yesterday
bus	examination	information	month	sound	
certain	except	January	morning	term	
certainly	February	July	must	think	
change	fifteen	June	national	thirty	

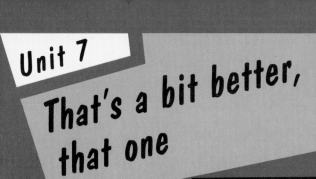

Unit 7
That's a bit better, that one

housewives

teenage boys who like riding bikes

people who use a home computer

people who are interested in birds, animals, flowers etc.

anyone interested in society today: how social life is changing, etc.

young men and women who work in London

people who want to take better photographs

teenage girls who are interested in fashion, pop music etc.

someone who wants a summary of the week's news

someone who is planning to buy something expensive and wants to know which make or model gives best value for money

nature INTERNATIONAL WEEKLY JOURNAL OF SCIENCE

Amateur Photographer WORLD'S BEST SELLING PHOTO WEEKLY

HOMES & GARDENS November 1986

NEW SOCIETY STOKE NEWINGTON TAKES UP ARMS

Your COMPUTER BRITAIN'S BIGGEST-SELLING HOME COMPUTER MAGAZINE

Which?

Time Out LONDON'S WEEKLY GUIDE OCTOBER 25-NOV 5 1986

THE PRICE OF OIL
OPEC After Yamani

Newsweek THE INTERNATIONAL NEWSMAGAZINE
The Way We Were
Our Ice Age Heritage: Language, Art, Fashions and the Family

Just Seventeen AUGUST 14 1985 45p Every Wednesday
City Slicker Special
FOOD for your face
THE BUSINESS

SHATTERED! UKBFA's ban on BMX BEAT coverage. Mega pix
BMX November 1986 N°46 85p

WIN! Holeshot Gear VIP tickets in our TRIP to AMERICA comp

DANGEROUS WORDS The Fanzine Explosion
DANGER! LIGHTS Ideas, dim products

Tyres
Long-life road-

AP COMPAC

Vivitar TREK 50 CLOSE-UP

How we tested the tyres

CREATING AN ILLUSION

THE JUST SEVENTEEN TERRIFICALLY USEFUL

LON DON

POSITIVELY JAM PACKED OF INFORMATION ON

- SHOPPING
- EATING
- NIGHTCLUBBING
- SURVIVING
- SPENDING MONEY
- SAVING MONEY

AND HAVING AN ALTOGETHER BRILLIANT TIME

LENS PERFORMANCE

95 | Magazines

What sort of people would buy each magazine?
What kind of things would they have in them?
Which pages come from which magazines?

What kind of magazines do you and your family and friends buy in your country?
Which magazines would you buy if you went to Great Britain? Or if you were staying in London?

96 Hairstyles

Bridget and David looked at these pictures in a magazine. They followed the instructions on the card on the right.

Look at the hairstyles in these magazines, and say what you think of each one.

Which do you personally like best? Do you like the same ones as your partner?

Which phrases did Bridget and David use about which picture? Can you guess?

pretty	*neat*	*very short*
too neat	*quite nice*	*too short*
very fashionable	*all right*	*not too tidy*
I quite like that one.	*horrible!*	*quite long*
I don't like that one.	*natural*	*a bit better*
That one would suit you!	*windswept*	

96 See if you were right.

▶ Did you agree with them? Tell the class about one style you agreed with David and Bridget about, and one style where you disagreed. ◀

97 *Wordpower*

look

Find all the phrases with the word **look**. Do you have the same word in your language for all these meanings?

Practise the short dialogues under the pictures. Which of them might you use yourself?

1

A: A lot of people are looking for houses in this area.

B: There are a lot of people looking for jobs, too.

A: Well, yes.

   A: What's the matter?

   B: I'm looking for Sarah.

2

Could you look after the children for me? I have to go out at 6.30.

3 The old man was looking at the newspaper.

   Take a good look and tell me if you see anything different.

Okay, let's have a look.

4 A: Do you know his phone number? B: No. Look it up in the phone book!

A: Excuse me, could I look up a word in your dictionary?

B: Sure.

5 look forward to hearing from you soon.
   Yours sincerely

6

A: Your hair looks nice.

B: Thank you.

A: What does he look like?

B: Well he's quite short and...

   She looked really happy.

7

A: Hey! Look out!

B: Oh thanks - phew he was going fast!

●ANGELA (21)

????: 'I'm a singer. I travel round with my boyfriend, Dave (that's him in the background). I make most of my clothes but I buy some second hand. My jacket cost £1.20, top £1.00 and skirt 50p to make.' *Shoes* Timpson's £2.00. *Ankle-warmers* market £1.00. *Dislikes* waiting for buses.

????: *Top* London (£22) *Jeans* from Manchester (£20). *Boots* Bertie (£50). 'I work as a surveyor, but I don't really enjoy it. I still go to college one day a week.' *Likes* music and sport: 'I like rugby, football, tennis, swimming, ski-ing, anything to do with sport.' *Dislikes* eggs and Saturday night discos.

●SUE (20)

●CHRIS (22)

????: *Jumpsuit* Miss Selfridge (£26). *Shoes* Dolcis (£8). 'I'm a window-dresser. I've been doing it since I was 16. I did this window behind me. I've been working here in Top Shop for 3 months. *Likes* window dressing 'It's the only thing I can do.' *Dislikes* unemployment and sausages.

????: 'I've come to Liverpool to stay with my parents for a week's holiday. I live in London.' *Dislikes* walking down Oxford Street on a Saturday – it's always so crowded. *Likes* sport. 'I play five-a-side football.' *Dress* Miss Selfridge (£16.99) *Belt* market (£3). *Shoes* Dolcis (£9.99). *Bag* Chelsea Girl (£3.99).

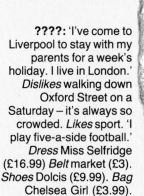

●JEANETTE (22)

a A magazine photographer went to Liverpool and talked to some young people there.

Which caption goes with which picture?

Which of the outfits do you like best? Put the pictures in order.

Who got the best bargain (the best clothes for the cheapest price)? Where from?

Make lists of their likes and dislikes. Put them into five categories: sport, food, work, personal things, other.

b Talk to other people in the class and find out what their likes and dislikes are. Write a list for each person.

Then put all the things into categories and tell the class how many people talked about each type.

c Interview one person and then write a report like the one in the magazine. You can ask questions like:

Can you tell me Would you tell me Tell me	where you work? where you bought your clothes (and how much for)? what sort of things you like.
Is there anything you don't like?	

99 *Grammar words*

with

1 together with
I travel round with my boyfriend, Dave.
. . . to Liverpool, to stay with my parents.

2 used to describe things or people
the man with blonde hair
the girls with the fish and chips

3 how
I'll buy it with my credit card.
Draw it with a ruler.

Make some sentences using **with** about the people on this page.

100 *Classroom language*

After class

S1: *We're going to see a film after class. Do you want to come with us?*
S2: *Yes please, I'd like to. Thanks!*

S2: *How much money do I need to bring?*
S1: *Oh, not much. About three pounds. Not more.*
S2: *That's all right then.*
S1: *See you after class!*

S1: *Alexos – do you want to come too?*
S3: *Oh, thanks, but I feel a bit tired. I think I'll go straight home. But thanks, anyway.*
S1: *Next time, maybe.*

101 *Grammar words*

to

Do you have the same word for all these uses of **to** in your language?

1 where
I've come to Liverpool to stay with my parents.

2 who (with **give, offer, present** etc.)
I gave it to David.

3 **listen** or **speak to** someone/something
Listen to Bridget.
Talk to your partner about...

4 purpose
I went to see my sister.
I've come to Liverpool to stay with my parents.

5 after **ask, want, plan** etc.
We asked people to write about...
It's for people who want to take better photographs.

6 after **it** (see **it** 2, section 88)
It was nice to see you.
When is it possible to phone your partner?

7 after **place, way, thing** etc.
What's the best way to travel?
London is a good place to live.

8 **from _____ to _____**
It was reduced from £25 to £5.
Our lesson lasts from _____ to _____ .

9 **used to, have (got) to, going to**
We've got to get seven differences.
David used to share a flat.
I had to come downstairs as the phone was ringing.

Which categories do these sentences belong to?

a *We only have to do seven.*
b *Say these words to your partner.*
c *Work in groups to do these puzzles.*
d *A man dressed as Napoleon went to see a psychiatrist.*
e *We're going to see a film after class.*
f *The cheapest thing to do is take a bus.*
g *Bridget works from Monday to Friday.*
h *I'd like to come back here.*
i *The psychiatrist asked her to sit down.*
j *Read these phrases to your partner.*
k *It's difficult to see the tree.*
l *He wants to go to Britain to learn more English.*

Compare the examples in each category with examples in the Grammar Book.

102 Shopping for clothes

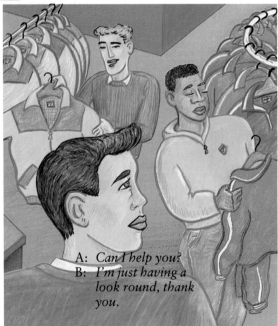

A: *Can I help you?*
B: *I'm just having a look round, thank you.*

B: *Can I try this on?*
A: *Of course. Over there...*
B: *Thank you.*

A: *Any good?*
B: *Maybe I'll think about it... and come back. Thank you.*

C: *Excuse me. Haven't you got these in another colour?*
A: *No, sorry. Only red.*
C: *Oh. Or this one in a larger size?*
A: *Very sorry, sir. We've only got what's there.*
C: *Oh well, never mind. Thanks anyway.*

103 *English sounds*

103a **a** What sound do the words in each set have in common?

1 dictionary, conversation, sure, shoes, station, fashionable, finish, international
2 cheapest, which, each, change, check, children, picture, French
3 jacket, January, Bridget, Jenny, orange, June, newsagents, just

103b **b** Listen for the words that are stressed.

What do you think of this one?
What do you think of the blue one?

I don't know.   *It's too short.*
I'm not sure.   *It's a bit too short.*
I quite like that one.   *It's a bit too short, that one.*

c Read this story. Which words do you think are stressed?

One day, I saw little identical twins wearing T-shirts. One child's shirt read: 'I'm Timmy. He's Tommy.' The other's said: 'I'm Tommy. He's Timmy.'

103c Listen for the stressed words.

Best bargains

> **bargain** something bought very cheap, especially in a shop sale

a Look at the pictures and read the text.

An Oxfam shop sells second hand things that are given to the shop, and also handicrafts made by people in the Third World. All the profits go to the charity 'Oxfam' which is a Famine Relief Agency based in Oxford. Oxfam shops are popular because they sell things at low prices and because the money goes to the poor in Third World countries. JC

Best and worst: Bridget's and David's best bargains, together with Bridget's worst buy.

b Can you guess:

Which item was the worst buy? Why?
Which was Bridget's best bargain, and which was David's?

▶ Write down what you guessed and then tell each other. ◀

Language study ···········

which, that, who

First fill in the blanks. Find the words **which** and **that** in the middle of sentences. Do **which** and **that** mean the same, or not?

a big man's jumper which started off at about _____ pounds,

My _____ was a shirt that I bought, and when I . . .

an enormous American Forces raincoat which I got from _____ for _____ pounds.

Yours was a man's jersey that you bought in a _____

The _____ thing – you've ever bought was a shirt . . .

Now look at these sentences. Find the words **which, that** and **who**. When do we use **who** and not **which**?

a *This was the outfit that Sue was wearing in Liverpool.*
b _____ *was the girl who made most of her clothes but bought some second hand.*
c *The shoes which she bought from Timpsons cost £2.*
d *She said she travelled round with her boyfriend who was called Dave.*
e *She was wearing a jumpsuit which she got from Miss Selfridge for £26.*

Compare the examples in this section with those in the Grammar Book.

---

c Listen to Bridget and David talking about their best bargains.
How much did they pay for them?
How much were the things reduced?
How much would these things normally be in your country?
What was Bridget's worst buy? Why?

	BRIDGET	DAVID
ITEM BOUGHT		
WHERE BOUGHT		
AMOUNT PAID		
REDUCED FROM		

d Read what a student (called Julian) wrote from memory after listening to Bridget and David talking about their best buys. How well did he remember?

> *David's best buy*
> David's best buy was a United States Air Force overcoat, which was reduced in price from £25 to £5. It was heavy and really warm, and in very good condition.

Your best bargains

Tell the other students in your group about the best bargain you ever bought.

▶ Write about your best buy. Say where you bought it, when, and what it was (or is) like. ◀

▶ Tell the rest of the class. ◀

As you listen to the others, you can write three words to help you remember about the things people talked about. Who got the best value for money?

▶ Write about someone else's best buy. ◀

a   a bit

Do you have the same word for **bit** for all these things in your language?

Can you open the window a bit, please?
I waited a bit, then the bus came.
I waited quite a bit, then the next bus came.

Where's that bit of paper?
Would you like another bit of bread? Or a bit more of this?

Tell me a bit about your family.

That's a bit better.
Oh dear, it's a bit too short.
A: The telephone call to the United States was a bit expensive. B: Yes, it was a bit more than I thought.

b   another

1 additional, one more
A: Do you want another one? B: No thanks, that's enough.
Oh, and another thing, have you got your keys with you?

2 different
A: Have you got this in another colour? Or this one in another size? B: Sorry, we don't have any other colours…

c   feel

1 personal feelings
I feel a bit tired.
I'm not feeling very well.
I felt so happy!

2 if you touch something
This feels a bit hard.

3 **feel like** = want to
Do you feel like coming to town with us?

d   too

1
The flat is too small for a big family like ours.
£45? That's too much!
Don't drink too much coffee. Or smoke too many cigarettes…
12 midnight? That's much too late.

2
A: I like that one. B: I like it too.
A: My name's Richard. B: Oh, I'm Richard too!
If you're going shopping, can I come too?

e   other

Sometimes **other** means one of two (or one of a pair).
Sometimes it means one or more of a lot of things or people.
Decide which example has which meaning.

1 *I like swimming and other water sports.*
2 *I buy Home and Garden and other things like that.*
3 *Talk to each other and find out about your partner's likes and dislikes.*
4 *A: There's only one biscuit. B: Well I'll have this half and you have the other half.*
5 *On the one hand it's very fashionable, but on the other hand, it's a bit too short.*
6 *A: This one? B: No, the other one.*
7 *Are there any others?*
8 *He talked to a lot of other people, as well as his family.*

f   good, better

Who is speaking?

His English is quite good now.
Is that a good book?
A: Oh the keys! B: Good thing you remembered them!
A: How are you today? B: A bit better, thanks. A: Good, sit down.
I took him to a good doctor and he got better quickly.

I'm looking for a better job.

I like Birmingham so much better than London.

We'd better go now. It's late.
You'd better not get home after 12 tonight!

It's better to learn to swim and ride a bike when you're young.
Smoking's not good for you.
It's better not to start smoking.

g   best

What phrases go with **best**? What words come after **best**?

That was the one I liked best.
What's the best way to do this?
What's the best thing to do now?

It was the best bargain I ever got.
The best place to go is…
A: …the best in the world? B: I should think so.

They did their best to finish the work before Saturday.

h   only

I like window dressing – it's the only thing I can do.
Sorry. Only red.
We've only got what's there.
Bargains! Only £1.99!
We only have to find seven differences.

Important words to remember (462 so far)

agree	cheap	kind	only	report	style
also	enjoy	little	order	short	sure
bad	fashionable	long	other	size	take
better	feel	magazine	others	society	to
bit	give	maybe	pay	someone	too
buy	good	music	per	sport	want
cent	interest	nature	price	still	warm

Unit 8
The working day

Work 1 physical or mental effort used to perform a task
Learning English is hard work.
2.1 a job or paid employment
Jane has left school. She has started work.
2.2 to do a job or paid employment.
She works five days a week.
3 the place where a job is done
She has lunch at work.

[108] **Work**

Discuss. Which people on this page:

are working?
are at work now?
have jobs?
don't get paid for working?

Myf Sinclair lives near Birmingham University. While her three children were small, Myf worked very hard. As her family have now left home, she is able to travel more, which she enjoys. However, when she's not away, she tends to be very busy all day, often with work she does at home.

Sue Purseglove: 'I don't work, – I'm not paid ... I've got a small baby, so I'm at home ...'
Sue used to be a teacher, but now with the baby, she finds she works even harder than before: 'It never ends! You just go on and on!'

Look at all the different people on this page. Which questions would be suitable for each of them?

What time do you leave for work?
What time do you start work?
What time do you finish work?
What hours do you work?
How long do you get for your lunch break?
Do you have a coffee break?
Do you ever have to work at weekends?

Do you take much time off?
What time do you start school/college/at the university?
When do you usually start your housework?

How do you get to work?
How do you get to college/the university/school?
How do you get to the shops?

Look at the dictionary definition above. Look at all the uses of the word **work** in this section and say whether they are used with meaning 1, 2, or 3.

45

109 Philip and Ken's day

Philip   Ken

Birmingham University   Bournville College

109a a You will hear Myf interviewing either Philip or Ken. Listen to find out which.
One of them is a student and one is a teacher. Which is which, and where do they each work or study?

Discuss who you think works harder, and who does the longer hours every day – Philip or Ken, the teacher or the student?

109b b Myf asks Philip and Ken about their working day. She begins by asking what time they start work in the morning.
Find out who works the longer hours.
Make a table like this one and fill in the times.
Do they both work at weekends?

	Philip	Ken
Starts		
Lunch break		
Finishes		
Evening		
TOTAL PER DAY (average)		
Weekends		

110 Your day

What different types of work do you do every day? Remember, work can mean housework or studying as well as doing a job. Work is something we have to do whether we like it or not. It involves an effort of some kind.

Find out which person in your group works the longest hours each day. Make yourself a table to fill in.

> Tell the class which person in your group works the hardest.
> Find out which person in your class works the longest hours.

> Write about one person in your class (not someone in your group). Say what they do, and what hours they work etc. Do not put their real name.

111 Grammar words

by

1 who/what did it
Do you think this would be said by a teacher?

2 how
She begins by asking what time they start.
I do my shopping by car.
I come to work by bus.

3 when
I've got to finish this by tomorrow.
It opens at eight, so I'm there by eight.

4 where
There's a phone box by the school.
It's over there by the post office.

___

Find examples for each category.

a *She starts by asking what time they begin work.*
b *She usually gets back home by 9 a.m.*
c *... handicrafts made by people in the Third World.*
d *Come and sit here by me.*
e *Guess what your partner's number is by asking 'Is it under 50...'*
f *I think I left it by the telephone.*
g *I have to finish this by tomorrow.*

Compare the examples in each category with the examples in the Grammar Book.

112 Classroom language

112

T: *Okay, can you do this for homework tonight?*
S: *I'm sorry, but can I do it tomorrow? I've got such a lot to do tonight.*

Do you think these sentences would be said by a teacher, or a student, or either?

Okay, you can go now.
What do we have to do for homework?
Can you hear the tape?
I'm sorry. I don't understand.
We're going to do some writing now.
Can I do it in my notebook?
Who can tell me the answer?
I can't see the board.
Don't do it now. We'll do it later.
Can I go home early today please?
Do we have to do it in our groups?
Can anybody remember?
It doesn't matter!
We haven't finished yet.

Myf's day

a What meals do British people have?

breakfast A meal that is eaten in the morning, usually before starting the day's work.	**supper** A meal eaten in the evening. Many British people call this meal 'tea' or 'dinner'.
lunch A meal that is eaten in the middle of the day.	**dinner** The main meal of the day. We have dinner at about midday or early in the evening.

Read this passage and say what meals Myf has, what time she eats them, and what time she goes to bed.

Myf usually gets up at 7 a.m., with a cup of tea to wake her up properly. She leaves home at 7.45 to reach the University at 8 a.m. for her daily swim in the pool there.

She usually gets back home by 9 a.m. Then she starts her housework. She does a lot of other things as well, like writing letters and gardening, and she often has to go out to see people at some point during the day.

She has a quick 'brunch'[1] mid-morning, and she likes to have an evening meal with the family between 6 p.m. and 7 p.m. Everyone helps clear away after dinner. By then it's about 7.15 or 7.30 p.m.

Myf likes to relax in the evenings, but sometimes she has a meeting she has to go to.

She aims[2] to be in bed early two or three times a week; at other times she goes to bed after midnight, but usually before 12.30.   JC

[1] *br*-eakfast + l-*unch* = **brunch**!   [2] **aims** = plans/tries

113b **b** You will hear four short extracts from a recording of Myf and Bob comparing their days. Can you hear the words that are missed out of the transcript?

there, often, things, any, actually (2), time, afraid

Morning
MS: I get up at about seven and I . . . get my swimming _____ and go off to the University pool and swim. It opens at eight, so I'm _____ by eight.

Lunchtime
MS: Erm . . . I don't always have lunch _____ . I quite often come back from swimming and have a sort of brunchy thing.

Evening
BB: Yes, I – I then join the family for an evening meal.
MS: Yes. Evening meal, yes.
BB: Erm . . . Which can be –
MS: What _____ is that?
BB: That's around, sort of quarter past six, half past six.
MS: Yes. We tend to have it . . . _____ time really, between six and seven.

Bedtime
MS: Well, I'm _____ we tend to be rather late birds _____ . Although I must admit, er, I try to keep it before midnight, but very _____ it's after midnight when we go to bed.

114 *Language study* ••••••••••••

usually, normally, generally, often, sometimes, never, most days/mornings/evenings

Which of these words and phrases mean the same?

Myf usually gets up about seven.
I usually start at about eight thirty and go through till five thirty.
Myf usually gets back at nine and then starts her housework.
She often has to go out to see people at some point during the day.
She normally reads or watches television in the evening.
My lunch break is generally one to two.
Seven to seven thirty I normally read or watch television.
She works every day except for Saturday and Sunday.
I never work at weekends.
I work most evenings, a couple of hours.
Myf sometimes has a meeting in the evening.
She goes to bed early two or three times a week.

Make a list of time phrases in these examples, and practise saying them. For example:

about seven, at some point, during the day

115 A reading puzzle – half a story

In the lift, but what floor?

a Half the class together read Part A on page 99. The other half of the class read Part B on page 100. You can all take notes to help you, but you can't write more than 10 words.

If you are an A person, find a B person. Without looking at your books, tell each other your half of the story. A people start first.

What is the problem?

b Can you write down the answer to the problem? Do you want to ask your teacher some more questions? Your teacher can only answer with the words 'Yes' or 'No'.

▷ Tell the class what you think is the best answer. ◁

116 *Wordpower*

get, got

a Look at the story about John and the lift on pages 99 and 100. See how many examples of the word **get** or **gets** you can find.
How many have the same meaning?
Write the sentences with **get** or **gets** in a list.

b Which picture do you think goes with each meaning?

1 **get in/to/on/off** etc.
He gets in the lift and he presses the button...
· Myf gets up at 7 a.m. and gets her swimming things on and...

2 **I've got**
I've got one sister called Rosemary.
Have you got Liz's phone number?

c Write down:

one thing you've got in your pocket or bag.
two things you've got to do this week.
two things your partner has got to do this week.
two things you got last time you went shopping.
how you get to your English lessons.
what time your partner gets up in the morning.
who gets the most letters in your partner's house.
what you get every minute of your life.

d Compare the sentences in each category with those in the Grammar Book.

3 **I've got to**
I've got to finish this by tomorrow.
How many have we got to get? Seven?

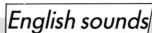

4 obtain/receive
Who got the best value for money?
The best bargain I ever got was a big man's jumper for five pounds.

5 become
Get ready to tell the class about it.
We got very tired after five miles of walking.

117 English sounds

117 What sound or sounds do each of these sets have in common?

1 work, swim, twelve, one, always, quarter, weekend, quite, want, world, when, would
2 were, thirty, first, research, surname, learn
3 work, world, worse, worst, word

118 Quickest in the morning

118a **a** Sue asks Myf, Philip and Ken some questions to find out what time they do things in the morning, and who is the quickest to get ready and leave the house.

Note down the times they get up and leave the house in the morning.

Work out which person is the quickest.

b Find out which person in your group is the quickest. (If you don't go out yourself, talk about a person in your house who does.)

▶ Write some sentences about the quickest person in your group. Don't write the name. Then tell the class. Can they guess who it is?

> X gets up at seven o'clock and leaves the house at seven thirty. So he takes only thirty minutes to get ready in the mornings. And that is with breakfast.

119 Inviting, accepting, refusing

119
A: *Are you doing anything this evening?*
B: *Well, I was going to do some jobs at home. Why?*
A: *There's a good film on. With Meryl Streep. Would you like to come with me?*
B: *Sounds okay. I like her. Yes, all right. That would be nice. What time?*

A: *Would you like to come out for a meal tonight?*
B: *Sorry, but I'm afraid I've got something on.*
A: *What about tomorrow?*
B: *Well, I've got some people coming round.*
A: *Oh, really? Er, what...*
B: *Yes, I'm awfully sorry. Thanks, anyway. Another time, maybe.*

120 *Grammar words*

at

1 where
The Hearst Ranch at San Simeon, California.
What time can you phone her at home?

1.1 in a place where something is happening
He's six. He's at school. (= he's studying)
He's not in. He's at the office. (= he's working)

2 when
It opens at eight.
I'm very busy at the moment.

3 look at, shout at, stare at (etc.) someone or something
Look at the photos.
It's very bad to shout at people.

4 at all (used to emphasise a negative)
We couldn't understand anything at all.
I'm not at all tired.

5 used to answer the question 'how much/old/fast/ often' etc.
The Hearst Ranch was built at a cost of US $30,000,000.
In Britain children start school at the age of five.

Say what category the word at belongs to in each of these sentences.

a *Philip is a research student at the University.*
b *Ken is usually at the college from nine to four thirty.*
c *He's very friendly. He always smiles at me.*
d *A: Are you busy? B: Not at all.*
e *They're selling radios at about twenty pounds.*
f *What are you looking at?*
g *I'll phone you at work.*
h *I never work at the weekend.*
i *Our house is very quiet at night.*
j *Jenny's not at home. She's at the cinema.*

49

a see

Sometimes the word **see** means to use one's eyes.

Look. Can you see the man with the brown hair?

But **see** has many other uses.

I go home at the weekend to see (visit) my parents.
I checked in Which? *magazine to see (find out) what the prices were.*

Look at these examples. When does **see** mean to use one's eyes?

Listen to the recording and see if you were right.
I can't see the board.
Close your books and see how much you can remember.
It was nice to see you.
We're going to see a film after class.
See you after class, then.
Could I see one of those please.

b Time phrases

Find the words **point, during, most, first, thing, once** and **while**.

While her three children were small, Myf worked very hard.
At some point during the morning we have a coffee break.
Myf always goes swimming first thing in the morning.
She swims once a day.
I work most evenings, but I never work at weekends.
Speak English during your English lessons and you will get better.

c any

1 The main meaning of **any** is 'It doesn't matter which . . .'.
A: *What would you like to drink?* B: *Anything, I don't mind.*
A: *When shall we go?* B: *Any time, it doesn't matter.*
Any child under 12 travels free!
Thanks, anyway.

1.1 It is often used in questions.
Can anyone remember?
Are you doing anything this evening?
Have you got any children?

2 It is often used after **not, never** etc., when it means 'none at all'.
I haven't got any brothers or sisters.
We never had any time to finish it.

Find the phrases with **any** and practise them.

I like rugby, football, ski-ing, anything to do with sport.
Come any time you like.
Did you find anyone with the same birthday as you?
I can't remember anything!
I don't like red. Do you have any other colour?
Have you got any money on you?
Any young person over 16 who is full-time at school or college can get a student card.
I'm looking for a job – any job would be okay. Anything at all.
New Society *– the magazine for anyone interested in society today.*

d nothing, no-one, nowhere, everyone, everything

A: *Nothing ever happens here.*
No-one ever comes to see us.
There's nowhere nice to go.
There's nothing good on telly.
Everyone else has gone away.
There's no-one to do things with . . .
Can't you think of something to do?
B: *Like what?*
A: *I don't know – anything . . . Everything here is so boring.*

e . . . else

It must be John – it can't be anyone else.
Sorry, I don't like coffee. Could I have something else please?
If there's someone else in the lift, he gets out at the 24th floor.
If there's no-one else, he gets out on the 14th.
Tea, coffee, sugar – what else do we need? Oh, milk.
John, Maria – who else shall we ask?

f main

Dinner is the main meal of the day.
The shops are on the main road.
The most important thing – the main thing is to speak more English!
The main meaning of the word 'any' is . . .

g able

As her family have now left home, Myf is able to travel more.
Sue is not able to work as a teacher now she has the baby.
Sue is no longer able to work.
I'm afraid I'm not able to come tomorrow. I'm very sorry.

To get to our place

122 Landmarks

When people ask us the way and we give them directions we usually use landmarks. We say things like this.

It's just past the hospital.
It's opposite St Joseph's school.
It's near the Post Office.
It's behind the supermarket.

Look at these landmarks. Do you know what they are?

Look at this picture. What can you see:

    just past the traffic lights?
    by the University entrance?
    on the left just before you get to the traffic lights?
    along North Road about fifty metres past the
       University on the right?
    just by the bus stop?

51

123 Street maps

Look at this small part of the *A–Z Street Map of Birmingham* and do this quiz.
Read the Reference section at the top of the map first.

Quiz

1 Which two postcode districts are on the map?

2 Name two main roads running from the south to the city centre in the north (one in each postcode district).

3 Find the three railway stations. How many of them are in district B30?

4 What is the name of the railway station with a post office nearby? Which one is close to a fire station?

5 Find Bournville Police Station. Which road is it on?

6 There are two churches on Bristol Road South. One is next to a post office. Where's the other one?

7 What is the name of the hospital on Bristol Road South opposite White Hill Lane? How far is that hospital from the nearest post office?

8 St Joseph's Primary School is just off Northfield Road. What school is on Northfield Road and is near to St Joseph's? (Northfield Road is in district B30, off Watford Road.)

9 Woodlands Park is between Mulberry Road and Heath Road. To get to it from St Joseph's Primary School you go along Northfield Road, then you turn right up Woodlands Park Road. As you cross Heath Road you will see Woodlands Park on the right. Where is the entrance to Woodlands Park? Is it:

a) off Mulberry Road?
b) off Woodlands Park Road?
c) off Heath Road?

124 *Language study*

a Look at questions 7–9 in section 123. Find the phrases which include these words. What do they all mean? Practise saying the phrases.

along, on, off, from, opposite, near to, in, between, up

b Look at question 9. What phrases follow the word **you**?

125 Visiting Philip

125a **a** Find out:
– what number bus Chris could get if he wanted to visit Philip.
– where the bus stop is.
– how far Philip's house is from the University.

125b **b** Philip tells Chris how to get to his house from the nearest bus stop. Chris draws a rough map as Philip talks.

Write down the landmarks Philip mentions.

125c **c** After Philip has finished, Chris checks to see if his map is correct. Did he make any mistakes?

Can you find Philip's road on the *A–Z* map in section 123?

127 Visiting Chris

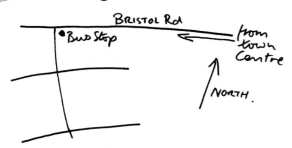

127a **a** Chris now tells Philip how to get to his house by bus, from the town centre. Philip draws a map to help him remember.
Can you find where Chris's house is?

Did Chris give good directions? What landmarks did he use?

127b **b** Now listen to Philip checking his map with Chris.

129 Following directions

a Look at the *A–Z* map in section 123.

Find Woodlands Park (in the middle of the map).
Go out of Woodlands Park and go straight across the road into Valley Parkway.
Go straight through Valley Parkway into Hole Lane and turn right.
Go up Hole Lane and turn right onto Mulberry Road.
Take the first turning on the right and then go into the first entrance on the left.

Where are you?

b Choose two places on the map that are quite close. Don't show your partner!
Tell your partner how to get from one place to the other. Your partner can use the *A–Z*.

130 Getting to your place

Student A tell student B how to get to your home from the nearest bus stop.
B draw a map without A seeing it.
A check the map. Is it accurate? Does B need to change it?

> Write short, clear directions to your partner's home and put these up on the wall. Put your map up too, but not next to the directions. Can other people match your directions to your map?

131 Wordpower

place

Place can mean either a general area, or somewhere specific.

1 a town or village
Stratford is an interesting place.

2 an area or district
There are some beautiful places just outside Manchester.

3 a seat or chair
Is this place taken?

4 a house or flat (informal)
Let's meet at my place.

5 a page or line in a book
I've lost my place.

6 a shop or restaurant
Yes, it's a good place, but it's very expensive.

Look at these examples and say if the word **place** has meaning 1, 2, 3, 4, 5 or 6.

a To get to my place, you take a number 53.

b There are some really nice places for walking in the North of England.

c Let's find a place to have a cup of coffee.

d Birmingham's quite a nice place to live.

e Excuse me, that's my place. Look, seat number J8.

f Okay, page 26. Have you found the place?

132 Grammar words

do

What is the difference between sets 1 and 2?

Set 1
Ask your teacher if you don't understand.
How do you know?
It doesn't matter.
What does Chris say?
I didn't get up until 8.30, so I was late.
Did Chris give good directions?

Set 2
I usually do the cooking and cleaning in the morning.
My husband does the gardening at weekends.
He did the meals when I was ill.
What are you doing?
All right. You do it first, then it's my turn.

These examples are a mixture of sets 1 and 2. Sometimes both types appear in the same sentence. Which is which?

a What does your brother do?
b Did you do your homework?
c No, I didn't, because I had a lot of other things to do.
d Who's going to do the dishes?
e Which bus? A 62 or 63 will do just as well.
f Is this yours? No, it's nothing to do with me.
g Have you done your homework?
h It doesn't matter.

Look at the Grammar Book. Which categories do the last eight examples go into?

133 Jenny and Bridget's education

What kinds of schools are there on the A–Z map in section 123?

Write down five questions you would ask if you wanted to find out about the system of education in another country.

Jenny and Bridget have written about their education. Find out at what age people in Britain:

start school
go to secondary school
go to a college of further education
leave school to start work
go on to advanced education
finish university

134 Language study

a there, where

Find four examples of the word **there** and three of the word **where** in the texts in section 133. What place do they refer to in each case?

b How long?

Find time phrases which tell us 'how long'. (For example: for five years, until I was eleven ...)
Write them down and practise saying them.

I started primary school at the age of almost four, at a private school in the Isle of White, where my father was working. Then we moved to Derbyshire, and I attended the village school for five years. My father then spent two years working as a missionary in the South Pacific, and of course we all went with him. I attended a small primary school there, until we returned to England. By this time I was already eleven. We stayed a short time with my grandparents in Suffolk, and I went to the local village school for a term. Then we moved to Staffordshire, and I spent a term at the state-run Secondary School, before being sent to a nearby boarding school. I stayed at the boarding school for seven years, and then I went to the University of Hull until I graduated three years later.

Jenny K

My Primary School was in Tunbridge Wells, Kent, and it was called Harecroft School. I was there until I was eleven and then I went to Wadhurst College. I stayed there for only one year, and then I left and went to the Sacred Heart School in Tunbridge Wells for four years, where I took by 'O' levels. My best subjects were French and English. I left school and went to St James' Secretarial College in London for one year. When I left there, I started working for Macmillan's Publishers where I stayed for one and a half years.

Bridget Green

1 a fee-paying girls' school

54

135 Your education

> **a** Write a paragraph about your education. Don't write as much as Bridget and Jenny did. Read each other's paragraphs. Try to find someone else who has had the same type of education as you.

b Find out when each member of your group left school and what they did.

> Write two or three sentences about one member of your group. Don't write their name. Give your sentences to your teacher.

136 Requesting directions

A: *Er, do you know where Green Park is?*
B: *I think it's down there somewhere, but I don't really know. Sorry.*
A: *Never mind, it doesn't matter.*

> C: *Er, Green Park?*
> D: *First on the left, down to the end. You'll see it!*
> C: *Thanks very much.*

137 Which sounds do the words in these sets have in common?

1 walk, quarter, floor, corner, important, small, normally, fourth, you're
2 phone box, sorry, across, off, opposite, stop, along, watch, clock
3 across, entrance, hundred, station, police, normally, Bristol, continue, another

138 | Grammar words |

can, could

(For meaning 1, **could** is usually the past tense of **can**. For meanings 2 and 3 **could** is usually a more formally polite form than **can**.)

1 ability/possibility
Can you follow these directions?
It must be John. It can't be anyone else.
I was so tired I couldn't stay awake.
What can you see from your classroom window?

1.1 **could** for suggestions
A: *What shall we do?* B: *We could go to the cinema.*
What about 1989? Could it be a telephone number?

2 permission
You can write three words to help you remember.
I asked if I could go home early.

3 offer/request
Can you open the window a bit please?
Could you open the window a bit please?
Can I help you?

Say if these sentences are expressing meanings 1, 2 or 3.
a *Close your books and see how much you can remember.*
b *You can go out now, but come back in ten minutes time.*
c *Do you think you could help?*
d *I can understand English but I can't speak very well.*
e *I can't come tomorrow. I've got a meeting.*
f *Can you spell that for me please?*
g *Can I carry that for you?*
h *The tape was so fast that we couldn't understand.*
i *That could be John.*
j *Can you hear me?*

Compare the examples in each category with those in the Grammar Book.

The expression **can be** is very common.
'Housework can be very hard work' means 'Housework is sometimes very hard work'.

What can you say about learning English?

Learning English can be . . .
interesting, easy, difficult, very difficult, hard work, very hard work, exciting, boring, horrible, enjoyable, fun, good fun

a of

Look at the Grammar Book. Which categories do these examples belong to?

None of the yellow shapes are squares.
I've got a couple of credit cards.
Go to the end of St Laurence Road.
Read the Reference section at the top of the map first.
Work in groups of three or four.
The twenty-fifth of December.
What's the name of the college?
A book of stories.
I felt sort of tired.
What sort of school was it? State-run or fee-paying?

b until, across, over, through, further/another, along, on

Find phrases with these words in the sentences below.

I didn't get up until 8.30 so I was late.
Go on until you come to the crossroads.
I was there until I was eleven.
I work from 8.30 till 5.30.
He looked across the river.
She went right across Europe by bus.
There's a bridge over the river.
The High Street goes right through the village.
I slept through the night.
They talked all through the meal.
You walk along a further fifty yards.
It's another two hundred yards.
You go on another mile or so.
It's a bit further on, on the right.
Some people leave school at sixteen and go on to a College of Further Education.

c up, down

1 Sometimes **up** and **down** mean the opposite (i.e. **up** = not down, **down** = not up).
Can you pick that up please?
Can you put it down, please?

2 But sometimes they mean almost the same. **Up** = **down** (e.g. along a road, street etc., even when it is quite flat).
Go down the road another fifty yards.
Go up the road another fifty yards.
Right up to the end of the road.
Right down to the end of the road.
Can you move up a bit please?

3 **up** = to, stopping there
He came up to me.
They walked up behind me and said 'Boo'.

4 **up** = not asleep, not in bed
I was up until 1.30 a.m.
We stayed up watching TV.

d exactly

Is his map exactly right?
A: What's the time? B: Exactly 3 o'clock.

e turn

Turn this way and look at me.
Turn left down Heath Road South.
Turn your books over so you can't see.
Turn the key this way to open the door.
Can you turn the light on please?
All right, you do it first, then it's my turn.

f off

1 with **go, start** etc.
Let's start off with you.
I get my swimming things and go off to the University.
He usually stops off at the shops to buy some sweets.

2 with **turn/switch** + **television/radio** etc.
The television set is on in picture A but off in picture B.
Can you turn that music off please?

3 next to
There's a front room with a kitchen off it.
St Joseph's Primary School is just off Northfield Road.

4 with **get/take** etc.
Get off the bus at Northfield Road.
Could you take those books off the table please?

g Expressions of distance

Where are you now? Can you think of places that are:

about five miles away?
about five minutes walk away?
less than five minutes by bus?
a bit more than a mile away?
about two hundred yards away?
200 metres further down the road?

h already

By this time I was already eleven.
Look! It's already midnight! We should go home.
Come and have lunch with us.
Thanks, but I've already eaten.

Important words to remember (550 so far)

across	city	entrance	mile	road	turn
along	corner	exactly	near	school	until
already	couple	fact	park	station	up
away	cross	far	pass	straight	walk
behind	direction	further	past	street	
centre	down	hospital	place	system	
check	education	into	police	through	
church	end	map	primary	traffic	

Unit 10
Revision Unit

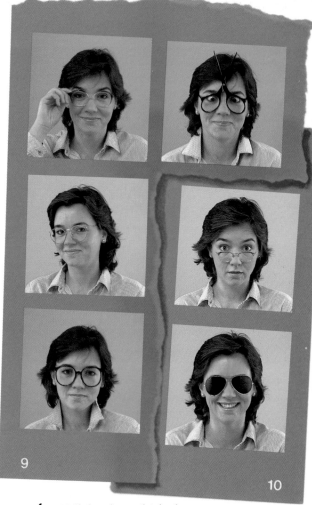

9

10

140 Glasses

a David and Bridget were asked to look at a magazine and discuss some pairs of glasses.

Decide which pair you think are best for this girl. Then decide which pair you think Bridget and David chose.

Which pair of glasses would you say were: severe? a bit too small? too heavy? ridiculous? really nice? neat?
– the round ones? – the dark ones? – the clear ones?

Say which pair you would choose for Bridget. Say why.
Decide which pair would suit you best.

b Tell the class which glasses:

– you thought were best for the girl in the picture.
– you think Bridget and David chose for the girl.
– you would choose for Bridget.
– you would choose for yourself, if you had to wear glasses and if you had to choose from these.

140c **c** Now see whether you agree with David and Bridget.

141 *Grammar words*

who, what, where, when, how etc.

after know, remember, tell, ask etc.

Practise sentences from this table.

Can you remember	where he lives	
Do you know	what he said	
Could you tell me	what our homework is	?
I know	where she was born	
I don't know	who that woman is	
I can't remember	who that was	
Ask him/her	how old he is	
I'll tell you	what he does	
	how many brothers he has	.
	how far it is	

Can you complete these sentences from memory?

Bridget lives in _____ .
David lives in _____ .
David's address is _____ .
Bridget's address is _____ .
Bridget is _____ years old.
David is _____ years old.
Bridget comes from _____ .
David comes from _____ .
Bridget has _____ brothers.
David has _____ sisters.

If you can, then say:

> *I know where Bridget lives.* etc.

If you can't, then say:

> *I don't know where Bridget lives.*
> or *I can't remember where Bridget lives.*
> or *Do you know how many sisters she has?*

142 Going to bed

142a **a** Jenny asked Danny, Bridget and David what time they normally went to bed.
Who would you think goes to bed the latest? Listen and find out.

b Find out what time the others in your group usually go to bed.

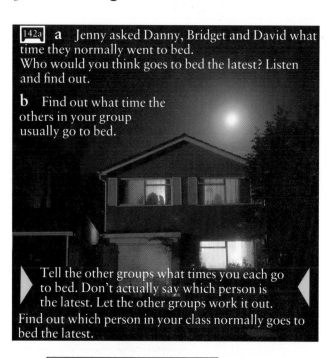

Tell the other groups what times you each go to bed. Don't actually say which person is the latest. Let the other groups work it out.
Find out which person in your class normally goes to bed the latest.

143 Game

The K and S Mystery Game

a For this game, instead of being called A and B students, you will be called K and S students.
This is because Ken and Sue also played this game, and after playing it yourselves you will listen to them.

If you are an S student go to your teacher for instructions.

If you are a K student, the S student will be asking you questions about things that you usually do during the day, and the times that you do them. Be as helpful as you can and answer the questions as fully as you can.

143b **b** How many things did Sue find out? Did you do better?

144 *Language study*

myself, yourself

Look at these examples, and try to find out when we say **myself** and not **me**, **yourself** and not **you** etc.

Danny is self-employed – he works for himself. He said to the others: 'I'm self-employed, I work for myself.'

David asked Bridget which glasses she would choose for herself. 'And which ones would you choose for everyday use for yourself?'
But Bridget didn't ask David which glasses he would choose for himself!

... after playing this game yourselves.
David lives by himself in a flat in London, but Bridget shares her flat with someone else. But both she and her flatmate look after themselves.

Other useful phrases:

She bought herself a new pair of shoes.
He made himself a cup of tea.
Have some more salad. Help yourselves!
I did the kitchen myself, and it looks quite nice.

145 Would you be a good witness?

a This photograph of a street in Farnham, Surrey was taken on 19th March 1984.
Look at this picture very carefully for one minute. Try to remember where people are standing or walking, what people are wearing, and what they look like. Look at the traffic, too. Remember in which direction the cars etc. are going, or where they are parked.

Working in groups, make some questions about the picture.

Close your books and ask the other groups your questions.

b Pretend you are one of the people in the picture. Write a description of what was happening at that point in time, from that person's point of view.
Give it to other students to read. Can they work out who you are?

There were some _____ passing me walking towards the _____. On my left was a _____ waiting to _____. In front of me was a house with _____.

146 A friend in common

Macmillan's London office

146a **a** What are David and Bridget trying to do in this recording? What questions do they ask each other?

Look at these pictures. They might give you some clues.

Listen to David and Bridget again. Try to remember the questions they ask.

b How many of these sentences are definitely true? How many might be true? How many are definitely not true?

1 *Both Bridget and David work full-time for Collins.*
2 *They both know Sarah, who works for Collins.*
3 *Macmillan is a publishing company that publishes magazines.*
4 *Bridget works for Macmillan as well as Collins.*
5 *Bridget used to work for Macmillan but she left there some time ago.*
6 *David has got a friend called Keith Welsby who works for Macmillan.*
7 *David knows some people who work at the BBC, for the English by Radio department.*
8 *David used to work for the BBC but doesn't work there now.*
9 *Bridget knows a few people who work at the BBC.*
10 *David's sister has a job in London; she works as an accountant for a company called Deloittes.*
11 *Neither Bridget nor David know anyone called Nigel.*

146a Play the recording again and check.

147 *Language study*

a Questions about people

DF: ... What does your brother do? and your sister? Do they have jobs in London?
BG: My sister's got a job in London.
DG: Where – What – Who does she work for?

Why did David say 'Where – What – Who ...'? What do you think he was going to say each time?

David asked Bridget eight different questions with the word **know** in them. Can you remember any of the questions that David used?
Try to write some down. Then listen to the recording again.

Repeat all the questions with **know** in them. Finally check the transcript.

b used to

When do we use the words **used to** with a verb?

In Unit 4, David talked about his new flat. Before he bought his new flat he used to live in a flat in the next street.

Sue used to be a teacher, but now she has a small baby so she doesn't go out to work any more.

Bridget used to work for Macmillan, but now she works for Collins. 'I used to work for Macmillan's, so I know some people there.'

 BBC English by radio

148 Your friends

Talk to someone in your class. Together find out if you have friends or relatives who:

have the same job.
work at the same place.
have the same first name.
live in the same street.
have the same birthday.

Write down the names of people you have found. Tell the class about them.

149 Students in your class

Look around at the people in your class. How much do you know about them?

Do you know where they all live?
Do you know where they all come from?
Can you remember where they lived before?
What can you remember about their families?
Can you remember when anyone's birthday is?
What do you know about their work? – Who works the hardest?
What else do you know?

Get into groups. Decide on the person in the class that you know most about (not someone in your group). Write as many true sentences about that person as you can. Don't write their name – just write 'he' or 'she'. Don't tell anybody outside your group who it is.

Put your sentences up on the walls for the others to read.

Go round and read all the other sets of sentences. Write down the names of the people you think the sentences are about.

a   to = in order to

Look at **to** in the Grammar Book. Which category do these sentences belong to?

Take notes to help you remember.
To get to my place, you . . .
Turn the key this way to open the door.
Quarter to eight I normally just get everything together in order to leave for college.
KO: At eight o'clock I'm just leaving the house. To come to work.

b   People: someone, everyone, no-one, anyone

[146a] Who says these phrases, David or Bridget?

The people here today . . .
You probably know everybody.
Do you know other people in the same business?
A few people.
So I know some people there.
Just think if I know anyone there.
Do you know somebody called . . .?
Do you know anyone at . . .?
Don't know anyone there.

c   instead

For this game, instead of being called A and B students you will be called K and S students.
Without the chips but with a salad instead . . .

d   just

Do you have one word for all these meanings of **just**?

1 only, simply
Just write 'he' or 'she', not their name.
I just get everything together. (the only thing I do is . . .)
PK: It's not a road, it's just an entrance to the park.

2 only a little; when used with a verb it makes it sound small and unimportant
just past the hospital
just before you get to the traffic lights
Let me just check that.
Can I just ask you something?

3 exactly
There's a telephone box just on the corner.
That map's just right.
At 8 a.m. I'm just leaving the house . . .
Mm – an ice-cream – just the thing for a hot day!

4 a short while ago
A: Do you want to have lunch with us? B: No thanks, I've just eaten mine.
I've just seen the director.

e   without

Student B must draw a map without A seeing it.
Tea without milk, please, but with sugar.
You can learn English without going to England, but it's not so easy.
Can I have mine without the chips, please, but with a salad instead?
They went without food for about three days.

f   enough

More coffee? – No, thanks, I've had enough.

Ask your partner:
If you borrowed my shoes, would they be big enough?
Is your house big enough for a party with 80 people?
Do you have enough money to buy a Mercedes?
Or enough for an old second-hand car?
Have you got enough time to help me with my homework after class?
Do you understand the word 'enough' now? Is that enough?

g   begin, start, end, stop, finish, over

How many phrases with **stop**, **end**, **finish** or **over** can you find? What comes before and after these expressions? How many phrases can you find meaning 'start' or 'begin'?

He stopped talking and began to eat.
Could you all stop talking? The programme's beginning now.
They just couldn't stop laughing.
The film begins at 6.15 tonight. It'll be over by 8.10.
When the News is over, we'll start supper.
A: Did you like the film? B: Well, at the beginning it was really good, but by the end it was just stupid.
A: When does the course begin? B: Erm, I think it starts in September, and ends in December.

Say which examples refer to the past and which to the future.

---

address am and are ask book can class come day different eight either eleven English example first five form four Friday friend from goodbye he hello her his I is know learn letter London look me meet Miss Monday Mr Mrs my name nice nine no not number of one or page people person phone photograph please read same Saturday say secretary seven she six student Sunday surname teacher tell ten this three Thursday today tomorrow tonight true Tuesday twelve two use Wednesday what where who word write yes you your about any baby big both boy brother but call carefully child daughter family father find finish get girl had have how husband it key list listen lot man many married mean money more mother office okay old our parent picture plan remember right shall sister small so son sorry start stop talk their they thing useful we which wife woman yeah young age all another arm bag because become between black blue body brown car carry clothes coffee colour course dark difference eye face foot forget French game glass green grey group hair hand hat head him hold lady language large left light middle mine neither next none nothing ones part pink red repeat second shape shoe show some sort square tea them there

Important words to remember (565 so far)

enough	himself	myself	themselves	without
few	instead	play	try	yourself
herself	itself	round	used	yourselves

building chair close common cost... ...n it its kitchen less live may mind modern most move much new n... ...s than the together very wall west window world yet army born d... ...er off on opposite outside paper paragraph problem radio reply s... ...tree war well after afternoon ago almost American April August be... ...double each easy England evening exact examination except Februa... ...nformation January July June just last level make March May migh... ...er over personal probably quarter ring September sir sound term thi... ...agree also bad better bit buy cent cheap enjoy fashionable feel give good interest kind little long magazine maybe music nature only order other others pay per price report short size society someone sport still style sure take to too want warm able actually afraid anyone anything anyway at bank begin by college dinner during early else every everyone everything ground hard job late leave lunch main matter meal normally often once point quick rather see sometimes supper tend then till university usually vary view work across along already away behind centre check church city corner couple cross direction down education end entrance exactly fact far further hospital into map mile near park pass past place police primary road school station straight street system through traffic turn until up walk enough few herself himself instead itself myself play round themselves try used without yourself yourselves business busy country drive government important labour law lie life meeting parliament particularly party political politician present press recently rest seem sleep social spend stay such travel trip village visit wrong Africa alive always America as autumn bell bottom Britain British century coast cold dead decide degree detail Europe even experience farm forest France happen here high hill history hot idea later let mountain never perhaps possible pretty put rain reason river root run Scotland sea season single sky spring state summer sun suppose top type weather will winter above again arrangement arrive been below future lose receive should soon therefore understand whether available daily emergency especially fire free hear help if instruction keep machine necessary power private public service situation speak telephone whatever while within air chance figure holiday hope however love miss set since towards

So that was quite a busy day

151   A day in the life of...

Find one person on this page who:

    went to three or more different places.
    went out in the evening.
    did some shopping.
    did a lot of housework.
    got a meal ready.
    got children ready for school.
    got papers ready for a meeting.
    got home late.
    got home very tired.

    took someone somewhere.
    took something somewhere.
    had a meeting.
    had no time for lunch.
    had time to have a rest.
    had an easy day.
    had a hectic day.
    seems to have a good social life.

Tell each other. For example:
I think it was the businessman's wife who got the children ready for school.

Andrea Drayton is a social worker. She works mainly with young families who have problems. This was a particularly busy day for her.

Gregory has just started a new business. His girlfriend, Sylvia, is hoping that it will do well. She phones him one day at the office...

152 David's busiest day

a David and Bridget talked to one another about days when they had been very busy.

Look at the pictures and say what you think David did.

b Read the sentences below. Try to guess whether they are *true* or *not true*.

1 *David's busiest day was a Monday.*
2 *He taught in three different schools that day.*
3 *He started work at nine o'clock.*
4 *He worked for four hours at the first school.*
5 *He went shopping before lunch.*
6 *He had to teach in another school at one o'clock.*
7 *That school was close to his home.*
8 *He then had to teach in a third school in the centre of London.*
9 *He finished work at 8.30 that night.*
10 *Some friends came to David's house for supper in the evening.*

152b Listen and make a list of the things that David did. How many things have you got on your list?

c Look at your list and make notes (not more than fifteen words) on another piece of paper.

▶ Using only your notes to help you, tell the class about David's day. Try to remember all the important things he did.
How many did you remember?

d Bridget also talked about David's day, but without taking notes.
She checked with David to see if she had remembered everything.
152d See if she used the same words that you wrote in your notes.
Did she remember all the important things?
She made one mistake. What was it?
Why did David say 'More or less. Yes'?

154 Your busiest day

Tell the others in your group about the busiest day you have had recently.

▶ Decide which of you had the busiest day of all. Write notes so that one of you can tell the class about it.

Listen to every group. Take notes as you listen. Find out who had the busiest day in the whole class.

▶ Write a clear summary of one person's busiest day (not someone in your group). Make sure you have remembered everything they did. Then check what you have written with other people who wrote about the same person, and finally with the person themselves.

▶ Write about your own most hectic day. Do not put your name.

Listen as your teacher reads. Can you guess who the writers are?

153 *Language study*

a When we talk, we divide our information up into short phrases.

DF: **Then** I went **home** / and on the way **home** I had to do a lot of **food** shopping / **Then** I had **lunch** / I **just** had time to have **lunch** / **Then** I went **out** again / I **went** to an**oth**er school / the **oth**er side of **Lon**don / where I **taught** from **four** to **six** / Then I had **half** an **hour** / to **get** from **that** school / **down** to an**oth**er school / in the **cen**tre of **Lon**don . . .

The bold type shows which words or parts of words are stressed. Look at these carefully and try to read these phrases in the way David said them.

153a Try again.

b Why does David use the word **then** so much?

A day in Sussex

Village pond, Lindfield, Sussex

Sussex is a large county to the south of London with beautiful countryside and quiet villages, particularly around the South Downs. On the coast the climate is always mild in winter, and towns like Worthing and Brighton are popular retirement places for the elderly.   EF

South Downs, East Sussex

House in Sussex woodland

a   Look at the pictures, and the words and phrases in the box.
Saturday was Bridget's busiest day recently. Can you guess what she did? Remember that Bridget works in London, and that she lives in a flat there.

> family aunt cousins lunch tea supper
> a walk shopping came over drove down to
> took them went to see/visited got home
>
> on Saturday morning at lunchtime after lunch
> then in the afternoon in the evening

 Write five sentences. For example:
On Saturday morning, she went to Sussex to see her cousins.

Read your sentences to the class. Did you guess the same things?

155a   See what Bridget actually did. Take short notes. How many things did you guess correctly?

Bridget uses the word **home** four times. Which place does it mean each time?

155b   **b**   David summarises Bridget's day in Sussex. Does Bridget agree with what he says?

Grammar words

have, had

1 possess
David has a small flat in London.

1.1 wear or carry with you
The girl in my picture has an orangey blouse.
We both have a calculator.

1.2 be related to
He has a sister in New York.

(For category 1 **have got** is more common.)

2 with a time (+ **to**)
The busiest day I've had recently was last Monday.
Then I had half an hour to get from that school down to another school.

3 food or drink
I just had time to have lunch – Then I went out again.
I had an egg for breakfast.
Would you like to have a drink?

4 **have to** (see **have got to** in section 116)
We only have to get seven.

5 **have** takes its meaning from the words that come after it
Have a look at these photos.
I'm very hot. I think I'll have a shower.

Write down:

one thing you have in your pocket or bag.
one thing your partner has.
two things you have to do this week.
two things your partner has to do this week.

Which categories do these phrases with **have** belong to? (Some sentences have two different types of **have**.)

a   *You had a short break before you had to get to the other side of London.*
b   *On the way home I had to do some shopping, and then I had lunch.*
c   *You look tired. Why don't you have a rest?*
d   *He had a good time in Paris.*
e   *We had a good week's holiday.*
f   *What did you have for lunch?*
g   *Does anyone have change for a pound?*
h   *Do you have any children?*
i   *Jenny has an office at home.*
j   *We had a good day yesterday.*

Compare the examples in each category with the examples in the Grammar Book. See also **have got** in section 116.

157 Home

People often talk about 'going home' or 'getting home'. They also talk about their 'home town'. Sometimes these are different places.

Bridget explained what she meant by 'home'. This is what she wrote:

> What do I call home?
> As a child, I lived in a village in Sussex with my parents, and I stayed there until I was sixteen. Then I left home and went to London to do a secretarial course, and I lived in a flat in London, but I often went home at weekends to Sussex. I then had two places I called 'home': one with my parents in Sussex, and one in London.

Another English person explained what he called home. His name was Julian Cooke, and he was in the middle of a 10,000 mile cycle trip round the world.

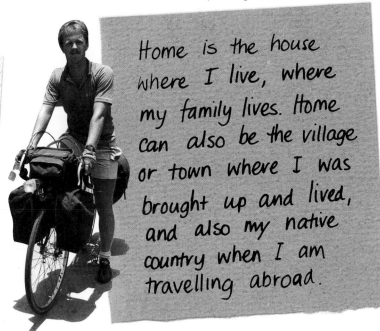

> Home is the house where I live, where my family lives. Home can also be the village or town where I was brought up and lived, and also my native country when I am travelling abroad.

So how many places does Julian call 'home' when he is travelling abroad?

What words do you have for **home** in your language? How many places do you call home? Is the place where you are living now your home? Or are you just staying there for a short time?

158 Puzzle

a How good are you at logical thinking? Can you work out this puzzle?

> Peter, Mary and John all went away last weekend. One of them went to Birmingham, one to Manchester, and one to London. One of them went to the theatre, one went to see a relative, and one went to buy a computer.
> Who did what?

Here are two clues to help you.

- One of them went to London to visit her mother.
- John bought a computer but not in Manchester.

	John	Mary	Peter
London			
Birmingham			
Manchester			
theatre			
relative			
computer			

Work with a partner. Write one true sentence about each person.
Can you explain to another pair how you did the puzzle?

> Tell the rest of the class who went where, and what they did.
> Then explain how you did the puzzle. Did you all do it the same way?

158b **b** See if you have the same answers as Bridget and David.

158c **c** Did Bridget and David do the puzzle in the same way as you?

159 Grammar words

go

1 move/travel
We'd better go now.

1.1 **go to/out (of)/back (to)** etc.
What time do you go out to work?
I'll have some lunch and go back to work.

1.2 **go and...**
Let's go and have some lunch.

2 **go to** = attend
I still go to college one day a week.

3 **go on** = continue
You go on another mile or so.
Don't stop – go on...

4 **going to**
It said on the radio it's going to rain.

Find out three of these things from your partner.

– where they went to school
– one thing they have got to do this week
– what they are going to do after the lesson
– how they go home after class

Compare your three sentences with the examples in the Grammar Book.

5 **go** takes its meaning from the words that come after it (**go for a...**, **go + -ing**)
Go for a picnic. *Go dancing.*

160 Story

This is a true story.

Mother at work

A friend of mine, a social worker, is the mother of five teenagers. In the middle of a particularly hectic week at work her eldest son, who was away at university, telephoned for a chat.

'What did you do at the weekend, son?' she asked with genuine but hurried interest. The reply came in injured tones: . . .

Write down the best last line you can think of.
Tell each other your last lines.

160 Find out what the last line actually was.

161 Finding more time

Write down two things that you like doing, but you never have time to do? (Lying in the sun, reading, or doing nothing?)

Write down two things that you feel you really *should* do, but you don't do because you never have time. (Writing letters?)

Show each other what you have written.

SORRY, BUT I JUST HAVEN'T GOT THE TIME TO...

What is the easiest way to find more time?

The easiest way to find time to do all the things you want to do is to . . .
Harold Smith

Can you finish Harold Smith's suggestion? Choose two or three of the following ideas. Then write one more idea of your own.

- stop chatting to friends on the telephone
- stop doing unnecessary housework
- buy a washing machine, dish washer, computer or word processor, or any other labour-saving device
- buy a faster car
- run to your meetings rather than walking
- work during your lunch breaks
- stop taking English lessons
- sleep less, or get up earlier
- do all your shopping in one go, once a month
- have less social life
- spend less time eating

Tell each other what you think is the easiest way to find more time.

Now turn to page 66 and read what Harold Smith recommends. Did any of you think of that?
Which is the best and easiest way? Take a class vote.

162 Wordpower

life

1 all the events that happen to people when they are alive
She has such a busy life that she always forgets my birthday.

2 the state of being alive
She risked her life to save mine.

3 the period that a person or living thing is alive
I've lived in the village all my life.

Which set of examples illustrates which meaning?

A Family life in West Africa is very different. And you have a very different kind of social life, too.
In real life, things like that just don't happen.

B There are people who spend their whole lives thinking about money.

DO YOU KNOW THIS MAN?

NEVER SEEN HIM IN MY LIFE!

C Listen, it's very important. It is a matter of life or death....
Is there life on Mars?
His son lost his life in a car accident.

SAVE A LIFE WEAR A HELMET

LIFE JACKET UNDER YOUR SEAT

163 Shirley Williams

Shirley Williams is one of Britain's best known women politicians. Born 54 years ago, the daughter of campaigning writer Vera Brittain, she joined the Labour Party and rose to the position of Secretary of State for Education and Science in 1976 before leaving the Labour Party to form the Social Democratic Party in 1981. Since then she has been in and out of Parliament and is chairman of the SDP. She is divorced and lives in a flat in Victoria.

Kathryn Brown interviewed Shirley Williams for a magazine a week after she had got back from a business trip to South America. Kathryn was asking her about her working week. Shirley Williams told Kathryn how she had spent one day.

Look at these pictures. Read the text on the right and say which order they should be in.

a

b

c

d

e

f

g

h

i

Tuesday

I got up at 7.45 and had my usual cup of tea and a slice of toast. Since my daughter Becky left home to go to college, I've had various people staying in her old room. At the moment, Becky's friend Stephen is staying, so I usually take him a cuppa in the morning. I went straight to the office and had a meeting on youth unemployment.

At 11.30 I attended a press conference at the House of Commons to talk about my trip to South America. I grabbed a sandwich and then I went to Imperial College for another meeting on unemployment.

In the evening I went to an IBM exhibition of advanced Computer Technology to see what effect it has on jobs. I got home at 9.30 and realised my flat was in desperate need of a clean and I had an important breakfast meeting the next morning. I was up until 2 a.m. scrubbing floors and dusting furniture.

164 *Language study*

Common phrases

The phrases in the box here can be used in place of the phrases that are underlined in the 'Tuesday' text above.

Say which phrases can be replaced with one of these phrases. For example, instead of **At the moment** you could say **At present**.

a big	visit
had a quick	stayed
went to	really needed cleaning
doing housework	find out
at present	
about young people out of work	

The last line of the story about the mother who was a social worker was: 'I was home for the weekend, Mum!'

The way to find more time is to turn off the television.

165 Stories about Esau

The name Esau is a very old fashioned boy's name. Both these stories are well-known among British children. They are so old that we don't know who first told them.

165a a I saw Esau sitting on a seesaw

One child said to another:
'Listen: "I saw Esau sitting on a seesaw" – how many S's in that?'
The other child thought for a minute, and, repeating the words to himself, said: 'One, two, three, and "seesaw", two S's, makes four, five . . .'
'Wrong!' said the first child. 'There aren't any S's in "that"!'

165b b Here's a rhyme.

I saw Esau sitting on a seesaw.
I saw Esau, 'e saw me.

How quickly can you say it?

166 *English sounds* ·············

166 Here are three sets of words from this Unit. Which sound do the words in each set have in common? Say the words to your partner.

1 staying, straight, 2 a.m., break, explain, away, April, take, came
2 busy, friends, puzzle, afterwards, he's a, visit, easy, magazine, because
3 recently, centre, spend, seen, it's a, starts, social, less, sandwiches

167 Apologies and excuses

167

A: *Did you bring my book back, Brian?*
B: *Oh, Laura, I'm sorry, I've forgotten it. I had such a lot to do last night . . .*
A: *Never mind, tomorrow will do.*
B: *Thanks, Laura.*

A: *Oh, you're back. Did you have a good day?*
B: *Yes, it was really interesting. We did so much, saw so many things and talked to such a lot of people . . . Why didn't you come?*
A: *Yes, I'm sorry, I couldn't. I had so much to do – just didn't have time . . .*

168 *Grammar words* ·············

that (look at section 76g)

1 pointing back (compare **it** 1, section 88)
That was a nice lesson.
Oh that's all right.

2 **that** person/thing
Is this yours? It was on that table, after class on Tuesday.

When **that** has meanings 1 or 2 it is pronounced /ðæt/.

3 after **say**, **know**, **hope**, **think** etc.
Greg's girlfriend is hoping that his business will do well.

4 **so that** for purpose/result
*Take notes so that you will remember **what** happened.*
I was so tired that I couldn't do my homework.

5 defining thing(s)/people etc.
Write down two things that you like doing.
Breakfast a meal that is eaten in the morning.

With meanings 3, 4 and 5 **that** is pronounced /ðət/.

That can be left out when:
a it has meaning 3 or 4.
b it has meaning 5 and is not followed by a verb.

Look at these examples. Put them into categories. Say whether **that** is pronounced /ðæt/ or /ðət/. Say if it can be left out.

a *I had half an hour to get from that school to another school.*
b *Write notes so that one of you can tell the class . . .*
c *Make a list of the things that David did.*
d *Yours was a man's jersey that you bought in a sale, that was reduced from thirty-five pounds.*
e *That's a good idea!*
f *David was so busy that he had to have a very quick lunch.*
g *That means that Peter went to the theatre, right?*
h *I don't like the glasses but I think that they suit her.*
i *It's a number 63. I think that's right.*

a take, took, taken

Do you have more than one word for **take** in your language?

1
Can you take some notes?
Let's take a break.
You must all take part in the discussion.
I don't take much interest in music.
Take turns to tell the class your story. You go first.
He took his exams last week. I hope he passes.
Take two tablets every six hours after food.

2
Take your books out. But don't forget to take them home.
I usually take him a cup of tea.
Please don't take the pencil away from the telephone.
He took his coat off and sat down.
He took her hand as they crossed the road.

2.1
Bridget's cousins came over and she took them shopping.
The social worker took Roger Beams to the clinic.
I don't take my children to school, they go by bus.
I've taken her to the doctor's twice, but she's still not better.
A: It's late. I'll take you home. B: Oh, okay, thanks.

b less

Find two pairs of sentences that mean roughly the same.

This one is less important, so leave it for now.
Social life is less important than a happy home life.
We have less social life than we used to.
We should spend less time eating.
He agreed to buy a less expensive car.
We don't have so much social life as we did.
Don't do this one now – it's not so important.

c stay

1
I didn't go out to work. I stayed at home when the children were small.
Jenny stayed on at school until she was eighteen.
Shirley Williams stayed up until 2 a.m. cleaning her flat.
I want to stay with my present company for another five years.

2
We stayed in a hotel for a couple of days.
Becky's friend Stephen was staying with Mrs Williams.

d such

It was such a nice evening that the children wanted a barbecue.
He had had such a busy day he was tired when he got home.
It was such bad weather we stayed at home.
We talked to such a lot of people . . .

e Time phrases

Last Monday
One Saturday recently
In the middle of a hectic week at work
Several years later
Until 2 a.m.
Straight after breakfast
And then
First thing in the morning

f home

Do you have the same word for each of these uses of the word **home**?

I went home.
On the way home I did the shopping.
When I got home, I had lunch.
I left home at 8.15 this morning.
I left home at the age of 16.
We've lived abroad for 12 years, but we'll be going home next year.
A: Where is your home? B: In the north of England, near Leeds.

g Government and politics

Shirley Williams is a politician.
She had the position of Secretary of State for Education and Science in the Labour Government from 1976 until 1979.
She helped to form a new political party, the SDP.

---

address am and are ask book can class come day different eight either eleven English example first five form four Friday friend from goodbye he hello her his I is know learn letter London look me meet Miss Monday Mr Mrs my name nice nine no not number of one or page people person phone photograph please read same Saturday say secretary seven she six student Sunday surname teacher tell ten this three Thursday today tomorrow tonight true Tuesday twelve two use Wednesday what where who word write yes you your about any baby big both boy brother but call carefully child daughter family father find finish get girl had have how husband it key list listen lot man many married mean money more mother office okay old our parent picture plan remember right shall sister small so son sorry start stop talk thank their they thing useful we which wife woman yeah young age all another arm bag because become between black blue body brown car carry clothes coffee colour course dark difference eye face foot forget French game glass green grey group hair hand hat he... second shape shoe show some sort square tea t... back bed borrow bring building chair close co... chen less live may mind modern most move mu... together very well west window world yet arr... opposite outside paper paragraph problem rac... well after afternoon ago almost American April ... ch easy England evening exact examination exc... n January July June just last level make March ... rsonal probably quarter ring September sir sou... o bad better bit buy cent cheap enjoy fashional... r price report short size society someone sport ... dinner during early else every everyone everyth... nes supper tend then till university usually vary view work across along already away behind centre check church city corner couple cross direction down education end entrance exactly fact far further hospital into map mile near park pass past place police primary road school station straight street system through traffic turn until up walk enough few herself himself instead itself myself play round themselves try used without yourself yourselves business busy country drive government important labour law lie life meeting parliament particularly party political politician present press recently rest seem sleep social spend stay such travel trip village visit Africa alive always America as autumn bell bottom Britain British century coast cold dead decide degree detail Europe even experience farm forest France happen here high hill history hot idea later let mountain never perhaps possible pretty put rain reason river roof run Scotland sea season single sky spring state summer sun suppose top type weather will winter above again arrangement arrive been below future lose receive should soon therefore understand whether available daily emergency especially fire free hear help if instruction keep machine necessary power private public service situation speak telephone whatever while within air chance figure holiday hope however love miss set since towards

Important words to remember (596 so far)

business	labour	particularly	recently	stay	wrong
busy	law	party	rest	such	
country	lie	political	seem	travel	
drive	life	politician	sleep	trip	
government	meeting	present	social	village	
important	parliament	press	spend	visit	

Unit 12

When I see a windmill I always think of Holland

170 Countries

a Where are these places? Have you ever been to any of them?

Africa (North/West Africa)	Holland
America (North/South America)	Japan
Australia	Spain
Austria	Saudi Arabia
Canada	Switzerland
China	Thailand
France	USA
Germany	USSR
Greece	

b Which photograph shows which place? How do you know?

How many of these can you find?

a big city
high mountains
flat roofs
nice blue sea
dry desert
bright blue sky
a lovely sunset
tall skyscrapers
some sort of temple
some tourists
a big vase
a windmill

c Do you agree with these statements? There are at least two about each of the last three pictures.

So that has to be somewhere – Mm . . . Can't be anywhere in Europe.
Well bits of the Andes look rather like that.
That looks a bit like the Grand Canyon to me.
We'll say Canada and we'll find out later on.
Okay, well let's say North America then.
Okay, let's say North Africa.
I don't suppose that it'll be New York.

d Write notes to remind yourselves which photo you thought was which place, and why. Were you quite sure about each one, or not so sure? (Write QS or NS next to each place.)

171 Do you agree?

171a **a** Which do Philip and Myf think the first four places are? See if you agree with them. (Philip and Myf might be wrong!) What were the main things they said about each photo?

Say which you thought the next three places were, and give a reason. Tell each other.

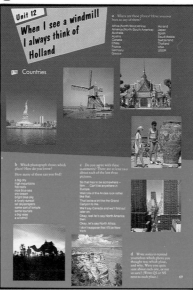

171b **b** See if you thought of the same places as Myf and Philip.
Which of the photos were the statements in section 170 actually about?

c Now for the last two pictures. In groups, decide which places from the list they could be.

▶ Write down the reason why you think so. ◀

▶ Tell the class your reasons. Take a vote. Which two places are they most likely to be? ◀

171c Do you agree with Myf and Philip? Did they both sound fairly certain they were right?

171d **d** With your notes in front of you, listen to Philip and Myf checking the answers.
Write down which place each picture actually was.
Who got the most places right, you or them?

172 *Language study*

a Expressing feelings

You can often tell how people feel about things by the way they say things.

172a Philip and Myf seemed happy with some of their answers, and not so happy with others. Can you tell from their voices how they felt?

Can you repeat the following phrases? The names of the countries are missing, but say them too.

MS: Good, that's easy. _____ _____, that's right.
PK: _____ _____, we were right. _____, you were right about that.
MS: _____, right. _____! Oh good!
PK: _____! Good. Oh, we know something then! _____, yes.
MS: _____. Oh it is _____ _____, see? Yes.
PK: Ah – The skyscrapers. Yeah. I think that – I think that is _____ _____.
MS: Yes. Yes.
PK: Mm.

MS: Erm. Yes. _____, this is.
PK: Oh – you know. Yes _____.

MS: How awful. Of course it is. Yes. Saint Ch- – the one up on the –
PK: Oh, on the hill. Yes, yes. Never mind. Right continent.
MS: Yes. And _____. So we got that wrong, that's terrible, isn't it?

PK: Never mind. I don't think we did too badly. I think getting _____ was good then.
MS: Mm.

b Reaching agreement

MS: Well when I see ... er ... a windmill I always think of Holland, so I would say Holland, for that.
PK: Mhm. Yes I think I agree with you.

Have they reached agreement that it is a picture of Holland?
Look what they go on to say. At which point do they actually reach agreement?

PK: Mhm. Yes I think I agree with you. It's flat as well isn't it?
MS: Yes.
PK: So it must be Holland.
MS: The –
PK: And the third one along the top?

171a How do they reach agreement on the other countries?

What will the neighbours say?

The day had been spent moving from our farmhouse in the country into our new house in town. Early next morning, our three-year-old ran into the room to wake us. I dressed him and told him to play outside and to stop bothering us. About twenty minutes later, he came running back. 'Mummy, Mummy,' he exclaimed, 'everybody has doorbells – _____
_____!'

a Read the stories and guess the last few words. Write them down.

▶ Tell each other your last lines. ◀

173a What are the last lines of these stories?

b Choose one cartoon below. Decide what you think will happen next. What do you think the people will say? And what will they do? Tell each other.

English spoken here

En route home from a recent holiday in France, I stayed overnight at a small hotel just south of Calais. On the wall by the entrance was a notice stating: 'ENGLISH SPOKEN HERE.'
Exercising my fractured French in the bar that evening, I asked the lady owner who it was in the hotel that spoke English. Leaning over towards me, she whispered confidentially, '_____!'

Anything exciting happen while we've been away?

I know, don't tell me, the Bensons are going on holiday and we've got their cat again.

Oh stop complaining, we'll just make room!

174 *Grammar words* ············

will, would

1 for fact or prediction (**would** is used as the past tense of **will**)
In ten years' time, Birmingham will be very different.
I knew Birmingham would be different.

2 for something imagined, not real (**would**)
We have to decide which glasses would suit her best.
Write down five questions you would ask if you wanted to find out about education in Britain.

3 to make an offer or announce a decision or promise (**would** is used as the past tense of **will**)
I'll phone you at work.
He promised he would phone me at work.

4 **would like** = want
Would you like a cup of tea?
I'd like to go to America one day.

Which category do these go into?

a *Stop complaining. We'll just make room!*
b *I agree. So we'll take the dark ones.*
c *I would go, but I don't have any time.*
d *I'll tell you how to get to my house.*
e *How many would you like?*
f *He said he would help us.*
g *Which examples would be useful if you went to Britain?*
h *If I have time I'll do it for you tomorrow.*
i *No tea thanks, but I'd like a cup of coffee.*
j *It will be nice to see you again.*

175 Seasons

How many seasons do you have in your country? Is it the same as in Great Britain, where there are four seasons?

Spring	March, April, May
Summer	June, July, August
Autumn	September, October, early November
Winter	late November, December, January, February

Sometimes spring is late and doesn't begin until late March or even April; and often at the beginning of September there is still nice summer weather. It varies from year to year.

▶ Tell the class about the seasons where you come from. ◀

Ask which is the best season in your partner's country? Why? What's the weather like then?

176 Welcome, or not?

a Bridget and a friend of hers, Carol, were asked to write replies to this letter. They had to imagine it was from a person they had met last year when they were abroad. This is part of the letter.

I might be able to stop off in Britain for a weekend on my way to or from the USA, in about six or eight weeks' time. It would be nice to meet again. Could I come and visit you? If I am able to stop off, any weekend around that time is all right with me. Just tell me when you are free. Please let me know as soon as possible, as I have to book my tickets very soon. As you know, this will be my first time in Britain, so I hope I can see you.

These are the replies they wrote. One of them is very welcoming, one of them is not at all welcoming, and one of them is fairly neutral. Read all three letters and decide which is which.

Dear Marcus,
Thank you for your letter telling me that you may be coming to England. Unfortunately, it will be a fairly busy time for us on the farm. As you know, we live in the country, so it would be very different from the big city you are used to. It will be in the middle of harvesting. I don't know whether you have had any experience with a combine harvester or a tractor, but at that time we will be out in the fields throughout the day.
If however the weather is wet we will be unable to do a lot of the work, and I may have time to show you the neighbourhood.

b Look at the letter to Judith. What words and phrases would you change or add in order to make it more welcoming? Write the letter out again.

Let others read your letter. Whose letter is the most welcoming?

Dear Judith,
Thank you very much for your letter. It is good to hear that you might be in England in a few weeks' time and it will be nice to see you again. I have no particular plans for the weekends around that time and will keep them free until I hear that you are definitely coming and on what dates.
As you know, I live in the country which is very muddy and wet at present. If by the time you arrive the weather has improved, and if you are fit for a lot of exercise, we can go for some walks and do some touring round the pretty towns and villages around us.
Best wishes, Carol

Dear Alison,

It would be lovely to see you in six or eight weeks' time when you are in Britain. Of course you must come and stay for a weekend in Sussex, or longer if you can make it. Bring lots of jumpers as it could be quite cold, and your walking boots as there are lots of super walks we could do. We might also play some tennis so bring your tracksuit and tennis shoes too if you have room in your suitcase!

Looking forward to seeing you again.

Yours,
Bridget

c Imagine that you had received a letter like this. Write a reply. Either welcome the person or try to put them off. You must be polite so that you don't offend the person.

as

1 as a ..., as the ...
As a child Bridget lived in Sussex.

2 as ... as
You can buy a house for perhaps *as little as £20,000.*

2.1 same as
Do *the same as* they did.

3 when, while
Listen to the tape *as you read.*

4 as if
It *looks as if* it could be in Greece.

5 because
I had to come down *as the phone was ringing.*

6 such as
Old towns, *such as York.*

7 as you know
As you know, we live in the country.

Which categories do these belong to?

a *He works for Barclays Bank, as an accountant.*
b *As her family have now left home, Myf is able to travel more.*
c *Write as soon as possible.*
d *It looks as if it might be in Spain.*
e *I often listen to the radio as I'm working.*
f *In hot countries, such as Egypt, ...*
g *Do you like the same ones as your partner?*
h *I lived in Africa as a young man.*

Compare the sentences in each category with those in the Grammar Book.

178 What countries?

Look at these photographs, discuss them and decide which countries they are.

Canada
China
France
Germany
Great Britain
Holland
Italy
Japan
Kuwait
Sweden
Switzerland
USA
USSR (Russia)

Find the following things in the pictures.

> a garden, a harbour, grape vines, a bridge, fishing boats, a valley, some mountains, some historic buildings, an area of forest, a café, a yacht marina

Get ready to tell the class which countries you think the photographs are, and why. For example:
We think the one with the grape vines is Italy, because they make a lot of wine in Italy.

▷ Now tell the class about some of the pictures. ◁

Take notes so that you remember what each group says.

179 The photographs

Read about the places in the pictures in section 178. Which description goes with which photograph? Find out how many countries you got right.

Glen Coe, in the Argyll Forest Park, Strathclyde.

Argyll Forest Park, Strathclyde, Scotland. This extensive area of forest, largely developed by the Forestry Commission, is less than 40 miles north-east of Glasgow, not far the famous Loch Lomond.

'Glen' is the Scottish word for 'valley'. The mountains on either side of this glen rise to 2580 feet, and can look quite alpine. At the top of the glen, at the height of 900 feet, there is a place called 'Rest and Be Thankful' where there used to be a rough stone seat bearing these words.

There are two camping grounds in the Park area.

Goodramgate – one of the 15th-century streets in the city of York, in the North of England.

York is for all time and every age. Renowned for its beauty, with a history that goes back two thousand years, it is the traditional centre of Yorkshire life and a place of almost pilgrimage for visitors all over the world.

Shipley Mill, West Sussex, near Horsham. Built in 1879, it is a fine example of an English windmill. It was working until fairly recently.

Windmills used to be quite common in the east of England; however very few are still in working order. Some have been converted into houses, but most are in a sad state of disrepair.

Mevagissey, a small, picturesque, fishing village in Cornwall, the most south westerly county in England.

Cornwall is a favourite place for British tourists from the Midlands and the north of England.

Vineyard at Cricks Green, Felstead, Essex.

Although most people think that Britain is too cold to grow grapes (everybody knows what the British weather is like), some varieties of grape grow extremely well in the UK. Even the Romans back in the first century AD used to grow grapes in Britain. Most of the grapes grown here are made into wine.

Brighton Marina, East Sussex, on the South coast.

Brighton is a lively seaside town with modern amenities such as excellent conference facilities and the lagest yacht marina in Western Europe. London is only 55 minutes away by train.

Early summer in the Chinese Garden, in Kew Gardens, London.

The Royal Botanical Gardens, Kew Road, Surrey. One of the greatest botanic gardens in the world, this has splendid specimens of all manner of plants, both outdoors and in tropical orchid and Australasian houses as well as the famous Palm House and the new Alpine House.

There is also a tall Chinese Pagoda in the Chinese Gardens at Kew. It was designed by Sir William Chambers (who had actually spent quite a few years in China) and built in 1761–1762.

With a total length of 6,156 feet or 1,877 metres (over water) and a single span of 3,300 feet (1,006 metres), Scotland's Forth Road Bridge was completed in 1964.

Even though the Forth River is only 66 miles (116 km.) long, by the time it reaches Edinburgh it is over 4 miles (7 km.) wide.

180 *Wordpower*

over

Which categories refer to time and which refer to place? Which don't refer to either?

1

Let's walk over the hills.

The Forth Bridge – a single span over water.

2 A: Where's Bill?

B: Over there by the door. I'll bring him over – wait!

3

There's been some difficulty over the children.

Their mother doesn't have much control over the two boys.

4 Over 400,000 people attended the New York pop concert.

5

Visitors from all over the world come to see York. They're famous all over the country.

Now try to work out the meaning of these words beginning with **over-**. Which category does each belong to?

6

Sorry everybody, but the party's over.

7

There'll be more problems over the next two years.

| overnight | overtime | overweight |
| overhead | overeating | overland |

181 Game

Twenty questions

A: *Okay, I've thought of a person.*
B: *Right. Is it a friend of yours?*
A: *No.*
B: *Is it a man or a woman?*
A: *A man.*
B: *Where does he live?*
A: *Sorry, I can't answer that. It has to be either a 'yes/no' question, or an 'either/or' question.*

B: *Oh, I see...*
A: *And you only have twenty chances to ask me questions*
B: *Only twenty?*
A: *Yes. And that makes four questions already!*

a Play Twenty Questions. Take turns to ask. Listen carefully to the answers, so you don't use up too many questions.

181b **b** See if you would ask the same questions as Bridget and Danny. Look at the card on the right.

182 Puzzle

Rachel was born in winter but her birthday is in summer.
How can this be?

182 Do the puzzle and then listen to David and Bridget's solution.

183 *Language study*

Isn't it? Don't they? Can you?

This type of question tag often comes at the end of a sentence, just before someone stops speaking. Look at the examples below and answer the two questions here.

1 Why do you think Philip and Myf use question tags?
2 How are question tags formed?

PK: It's flat as well isn't it?
MS: Yes.

PK: It looks a bit like New York, doesn't it?
MS: Mm. Shall we say, but shall we say a different one?

MS: It could be Egypt, or the Arab countries couldn't it? Tunisia.
PK: North Africa? North Africa.

MS: You've been to South America haven't you?
PK: That's right, yes.

PK: I don't think it's South America.
MS: You don't?
PK: No. I think it's North. North America.

MS: You can't tell anything from the people there can you? No, they're too small.

PK: But most photographs have always bright bright blue sky, don't they?

MS: We were wrong there then because we put Canada, didn't we? Or did we?
PK: We said Canada... No, we put North America.

Do you have question tags in your language? If not, what do you have instead?

Put five of these questions in the best order.

1 Is it a man or a woman?
2 Is it a pop singer?
3 Is it our teacher?
4 Is he/she alive or dead?
5 Do you like him or her?
6 Is he/she American or British?

Now think of three or four other questions you think might be useful, and write them down.

Tell your partner which order you have put the questions in. Find out if your partner has the same order. Find out what other questions people thought of.

184 *English sounds*

/t/ and /d/ sounds

a People always say T at the beginning of a word: **top, tourist, tell** etc.
But they don't always say T at the end of the word.

184a Listen to these extracts from the recording in section 171. When can you hear the T, and when not?

What about the one here at the top?
I don't know enough about it to say...
It's flat as well, isn't it?
So it must be Holland.
Not too sure about that.   *That sort of roof.*
It looks a bit like New York.   *Oriental definitely.*

b What about these Ds? How are they said?

trying to decide   *in the middle*
What do you think of...   *the third one*
I would say Holland   *It could be...*

184b Listen and check.

184c **c** Do these Ds sound like /d/ or /t/?

tourists dressed for summer   *She's divorced.*
He's married and has two boys.   *He said okay.*
She told him to go out to play.
She asked him to go out to play.

185 Making suggestions

A: *Hi Gill! What about coming out for the day tomorrow?*
B: *We're going up into the hills, walking.*
C: *Great idea! Who's going?*
B: *Oh, a whole crowd of us. Do come!*
C: *All right. What time?*
A: *I'll phone you later and give you all the details.*
C: *Thanks.*

a Ways of suggesting things

Let's put Spain.
Let's walk over the hills.
Shall we say Canada, because I'm sure they have...
Okay. Well, shall we take a look at the answer key now?
Why don't we have a day out somewhere?
What about coming out for the day tomorrow?
Perhaps we could have the windows closed – it's a bit cold.
If you would like to sit here...

b even

Sometimes spring doesn't begin until late March or even April.
Even though the Forth River is only 66 miles (116 km.) long, by the time it reaches Edinburgh it is over 4 miles (7 km.) wide.
... nice day? Awful! Didn't even have time to have lunch!
We'll still go out, even if it rains.
A tiny flat in London could cost £50,000, or even more!

c here, there

Do **here** and **there** always mean 'in this/that place'?

I haven't been there, but it looks very much like the photographs.
I think we toss a coin here.
Ah, here we are.
What about the one in the middle here at the top?
But the flat tops here. They're not like the Andes.
New York! We were wrong there then because we put Canada.
English spoken here.

d into

He ran into the room.
We moved into a new house.
The grapes are made into wine.
Some windmills have been converted into houses.
He changed into some old clothes.
England is divided into counties, like Sussex, and Norfolk.
Divide into two groups.

e perhaps

Somewhere oriental perhaps?
Where's Gill? Perhaps she's not well.
Perhaps we could start now.
Perhaps you could help me with something?

f possible

Anything is possible...
As soon as possible, please.
I'd like my coffee black, if possible.
Could we possibly have the window open?

g put

When does **put** mean 'say' or 'write'?

Can you put your pens down, please?
I'll put the money over here.
A: Shall I put your name down? B: What for?
Did we put Canada or North America?
We put Canada, didn't we?
Bridget put number one first.
How shall I put it?
Carol wrote a letter to put Marcus off coming to see her.

h think, suppose, tell, know and -n't

Study the phrases these words appear in.

Find the verbs ending in **-n't**. Notice where the negative comes in the sentence.

I think that's North Africa... I don't think it's anywhere else that's on the list.
We think of Holland as being very flat.
I thought of him not as a teacher but as a friend.
I don't think it's North America.
The child thought for some time, and then said...
I don't suppose that it'll be New York.
I don't suppose so.
You can't tell anything from the people there can you? No, they're too small.
MS: Switzerland or Austria... I don't know how you'd tell which one. PK: I don't know if you can tell, unless you recognise the actual mountain... MS: No. Which I don't actually.
Don't know where that would be in Spain.
I don't know enough about it to say it's China.

i state

1
The United States of America
Shirley Williams used to be Secretary of State.
state schools in Britain
a one-party state

2
He was in a bad state of health.
Most windmills are in a sad state of disrepair.

address am and are ask book can class come day different eight either eleven English example first five form four Friday friend from goodbye he hello her his I is know learn letter London look me meet Miss Monday Mr Mrs my name nice nine no not number of one or page people person phone photograph please read same Saturday say secretary seven she six student Sunday surname teacher tell ten this three Thursday today tomorrow tonight true Tuesday twelve two use Wednesday what where who word write yes you your about any baby big both boy brother but call carefully child daughter family father find finish get girl had have how husband it key list listen lot man many married mean money more mother office okay old our parent picture plan remember right shall sist... age all another arm bag because become between... h game glass green grey group hair hand hat head... second shape shoe show some sort square tea the... back bed borrow bring building chair close comm... chen less live may mind modern most move much... together very wall west window world yet army... opposite outside paper paragraph problem radio... well after afternoon ago almost American April Au... n January July June just exact examination excep... rsonal probably quarter last level make March Ma... o bad better bit buy cent ring September sir sound... r price report short size cheap enjoy fashionable... dinner during early else society someone sport sti... es supper tend then till every everyone everything... education end entrance university usually vary vie... hrough traffic turn until exactly fact far further h... ess busy country drive up walk enough few he... n sleep social spend stay government important la... such travel trip village visit wrong Africa alive always America as autumn bell bottom Britain British century coast cold dead decide degree detail Europe even experience say farm forest France happen here high hill history hot idea later let mountain never perhaps possible pretty put rain reason river roof run Scotland sea season single sky spring state summer sun suppose top type weather will winter above again arrangement arrive been below future lose receive should soon therefore understand whether available daily emergency especially fire free hear help if instruction keep machine necessary power private public service situation speak telephone whatever while within air chance figure holiday hope however love miss set since towards

Important words to remember (654 so far)

Africa	century	farm	later	river	summer
alive	coast	forest	let	roof	sun
always	cold	France	mountain	run	suppose
America	dead	happen	never	Scotland	top
as	decide	here	perhaps	sea	type
autumn	degree	high	possible	season	weather
bell	details	hill	pretty	single	will
bottom	Europe	history	put	sky	winter
Britain	even	hot	rain	spring	
British	experience	idea	reason	state	

Have you got any plans?

187 Plans for next week

a Look at what these people are doing.
How many of these things are you definitely going to do in the next week?
Which things do you think you might do?

Make a list of four things, and then find other people who are going to do each of them in the next week.

▶ Write down what you have found and tell the class. ◀

b What sports are these things used for?
Which of these sports do you do?
Which are you going to do in the next week?

billiards

skiing

squash

football

hockey

jogging

cricket

riding

weightlifting

golf

tennis

table tennis

cycling

77

188 Will your paths cross?

a Bridget and David know that they both use the same supermarket, Nisa in Notting Hill.
They tried to find out if their paths would cross in the next week.

188a Make a list of the things they are going to do.
Do you think their paths will cross?

Will you be going to the same place at all?

Will you be going to the same place at the same time?

b Make a list of the things you plan to do over the next week.
Try to find other people in the class whose paths might cross yours next week.

▶ Make notes, and then tell the class what you are going to do and if you are going to cross anyone's path. ◀

c Ken played a guessing game with a friend. He knew she was going to do one of these things the next weekend, but he did not know which one.

> go to a cricket match
> write a lot of letters
> catch up with work
> have friends for dinner
> have lunch with the family (parents/brother/sister)
> play squash
> have dinner out with friends
> play tennis
> go out somewhere for a walk
> watch video with family and friends

Ken was allowed to ask four questions. What four questions would you ask if you were him? For example:
Are you going to do this thing alone?

▶ Work in a group to decide the four best questions and write them down. ◀

188c What questions did Ken ask? Did he get the answer in four questions?

Did you think of the same questions as Ken?

d Play the same game yourselves.

189 *Wordpower*

see

What does the word **see** mean?

Bridget says 'I'll just see what happens.'
What does she mean?

1 you see (in conversation, when you are explaining something)

First, you see, you have to put the money in.

2 understand what is happening or agree with what someone is saying

I see what you mean.

A: First, you see, you have to put the money in. B: Yes. I see.

3.1 know, by using your eyes, what something is or looks like
3.2 to look at something carefully
3.3 to watch a film or play

When I see a windmill I always think of Holland.

DF: What are you going to see?
BG: Tina Turner.

4 notice (not with the eyes)

I could see that Jenny was unhappy at that school.

5 meet someone and talk to them

I would love to see you again.

6 discover or find out something

I'll just see what happens.

Look at these ten examples. How many of them have meaning 3?

a Let's see if we're right.
b They're too small. You can't see them clearly.
c Please come and see us when you are in Britain.
d See you after class.
e Go on until you see Barclay's Bank on the right.
f I checked in Which? magazine to see what the prices were.
g You see it's very important to find the right make and model.
h What does 'difficult' mean? It's the opposite of 'easy'. I see. How do you spell it?
i I saw a good programme on TV last night.
j I don't quite see what you mean.

Which examples go with which pictures?

190 Tina Turner

Tina Turner talks about her plans for the future.

Now – after appearing in Mel Gibson's film **Mad Max: Beyond Thunderdome** – Tina admits: 'The next thing I'm determined to win is an Oscar and – believe me – I'll <u>get</u> one.
'I've wanted to act for <u>a very, long time</u> but I had to master my singing career first.
'... It's the <u>most sensational</u> feeling in the world to <u>make</u> it to the top,' says Tina, 'and to know that you've done it <u>completely by</u> <u>yourself.</u>
'I know that many people didn't have any faith in me six or seven years ago. But I knew I could make it, I knew I would make it – and I have made it.
'After so much <u>hassle</u>,' grins Tina, 'I'm determined to stay at the top.
'At my age, I <u>reckon</u> I've got a good five or six years ahead of me at least.'

These words could be used to replace the words which are underlined. Where would they go?

ages, all on your own, get, greatest, think, trouble, win

191 Long-term plans

We make plans for tomorrow or next week, but we also make long-term plans, plans for the future.

191a **a** David asked Bridget about her job and about her plans for the future.
What does Bridget say about her future? Are there going to be any changes in the near future?

b Think of questions you could ask about your partner's future plans.

Try to find out three ways in which your partner's life is likely to change in the future.

> Tell the class what you have found. Listen and take notes so you will remember about the others.

> **c** Choose two people from your class with very different plans for the future. Write two or three sentences about their future lives without saying who they are.
> Let your teacher read the sentences to the class. Can you remember who all the sentences are about?

192 *Language study*

Talking about the future

Find the verbs in this transcript.
Find all the verbs which refer to the future. How many different ways of referring to the future are there?

DF: Will your paths cross? What about this coming week and weekend? Will you be going to the, er, Nisa this weekend?
BG: Probably, yes.
DF: Er, I might be as well, so that's a possibility. Erm ... are you going to the th- – Are are you going out this weekend to anything? Have you got any plans?
BG: Erm, I'm staying in London. I'm going to a concert on Saturday night.
DF: Where? Where's that?
BG: At Wembley.
DF: Uhuh. What are you going to see?
BG: Tina Turner.
DF: Uhuh. Great!
BG: Erm ... Then I'm going out to lunch on Sunday.
DF: Where are you going out to lunch?
BG: Parson's Green.

DF: Ah. I'm going out to lunch in Putney, which is close-ish. After that?
BG: Erm ... I don't know. I haven't really got anything else planned.
DF: So what about shopping?
BG: Oh, I'll probably – I'll have to go shopping at some stage, probably on Saturday.

Say whether these sentences are about the present or the future.

a *Are you going to play tennis?*
b *For the time being I'm happy.*
c *I'll just see what happens.*
d *I am writing with regard to my travel arrangements.*
e *Are you planning to stay with a friend?*
f *If you come home tomorrow I won't be here.*
g *Which examples would be useful if you went to Britain?*
h *Take a good look and tell me if you see anything different.*

193 Making arrangements

Every year there is a big international seminar at the Regional Language Centre in Singapore. People go to Singapore from all over the world to talk about teaching and learning languages. The British Council helps British participants by helping to pay their expenses so that they can attend the Seminar.

Letter from Singapore to the participants

The British Council

Promoting cultural, educational
and technical co-operation between
Britain and other countries

Singapore Rubber House
14 Collyer Quay, Singapore 0104
Telephone 5337644
Telex BRICO RS20456

Our ref SNG/0520/4
Your ref

February 19th 1985

Dear

I would like to confirm that the British Council Singapore will contribute £500 towards your visit to this year's RELC Seminar. Our Specialist Tours Department should contact you within a week or so with details of payment.

Please let me know as soon as you have fixed your travel plans so that I can make sure you are properly looked after on arrival.

I look forward to seeing you in April.

Yours sincerely

Dr J D Willis

Reply 1

ELI
English Language Institute
The University of Michigan
Ann Arbor
48109

The British Council
Singapore Rubber House
14 Collyer Quay
Singapore 0104

March 5, 1985

Dear Dave,

Thanks for your letters - an interim report from me. I am planning to make arrangements to arrive on Sunday April 21st and to leave either p.m. April 30th or a.m. May 1st. I have been in touch with British Council Washington about the payment of my ticket and I am hoping to finalise those details this week.

I do not know yet whether I shall be staying with Vijay Bhatia. I'll let you know as soon as I have heard from him.

Warmest regards to both you and Jane.

John Swales

TELEX WEXAS INTERNATIONAL

BOOKING NO. 002027   WEEK NO. 16
DATE 20 MAR

PROF J. MERRITT   COST
                              ST   D/BKD
                    DEP   ARR   485.0

CL DATE   APT TO   OK   20MAR
    18APR LHR AMM 0855 1740   20MAR
    18APR AMM SIN 2100 1350+1 WL 20MAR
Y   04MAY SIN AMM 0530 1045 WL 20MAR
Y   04MAY AMM LHR 1200 1710 OK 20MAR

The British C...

...yer Quay, Singapore 0104
Telephone 5337644
Telex BRICO RS20456

Dr M. L. Tickoo
SEAMEO Regional Language Centre
30 Orange Grove Road
Singapore

Dear Makhan,

I have just received this from John Merritt. If I understand it correctly he is arriving by Royal Jordanian Airlines Flight 182 at 1350 hrs on April 19th.

Yours sincerely,

Dave.

Dr J D Willis
English Language Officer

Reply 3

Reply 2

THE OPEN UNIVERSITY

SCHOOL OF EDUCATION
The Open University,
Walton Hall,
Milton Keynes,
MK7 6AA.
Telephone: Milton Keynes (0908) 74066
Direct line: 0908 65

Dr. J. M. Bynner
Dean and Director of Studies

Dr. Makhan L. Tickoo,
Chairman,
Seminar Planning Committee,
Regional Planning Committee,
30 Orange Grove Road,
Singapore 1025

28th March 1985
JEM/MVB/85/635

Dear Dr. Tickoo,

SEAMEO Language Seminar 1985

I am writing with regard to my travelling arrangements for the above Seminar. I shall be travelling by Jordanian Airways and should arrive in Singapore at 13.50 on 18th April. The return booking is for 05.30 on 4th May.

I have not yet got confirmation of the arrangements for the Amman-Singapore section of the journey so I shall have to confirm these timings as soon as I receive further information.

I look forward to seeing you next month.

Yours sincerely,

J. E. Merritt
Professor of Teacher Education

c.c. Dr J. D. Willis, English Language Officer,
British Council, Singapore.

194 *Language study*

Look at this extract from John Swales's letter.

*I do not know **yet whether I** shall be staying **with** Vijay Bhatia. I'll let you know **as soon as I** have heard **from him.***

Do the highlighted words refer to the past, the present or the future?

In Professor Merritt's letter there are four ways of referring to the future. Can you find them?

a Read through the letters and the telex and say whether these statements are *true* or *not true*.

1 *John Swales is a friend of the Willises.*
2 *Dave Willis knows Dr Tickoo well.*
3 *Professor Merritt is a friend of Dr Tickoo's.*
4 *John Swales is going to stay with Vijay Bhatia.*
5 *He is going to stay in Singapore for more than a week.*
6 *The British Council has an office in Ann Arbor, Michigan.*
7 *It will cost Professor Merritt more than £500 to fly to Singapore.*
8 *Professor Merritt is arriving in Singapore on April 18th.*
9 *He will have to wait in Amman for almost three hours.*
10 *He will be staying in Singapore for longer than John Swales.*

b Work out the answers to these problems.

1 There is a time difference of eight hours between London and Singapore.
What is the flying time between London and Singapore?

2 The RELC seminar starts on a Monday and finishes on a Friday.
Can you work out the exact dates?

3 On the telex the flights between London and Amman are marked OK, and those between London and Singapore are marked WL.
Why? What do you think WL means?

---

195 ## Grammar words

have

The words **have** and **has** are used to form the present perfect tense. This has three main uses.

1 for something that has or has not happened up to now
I haven't even been there a year yet. (up to now)
I've been learning English for a year.

2 for something that happened or did not happen in the past, but is important now
I knew I would make it to the top and I have made it. (now I am at the top)
I have not yet got confirmation of the arrangements for the Amman–Singapore section of the journey. (so I can't tell you about it now)

3 for something that will have happened at some time in the future
I don't know yet whether I shall be staying with Vijay Bhatia. I shall let you know as soon as I have heard from him.

Two of these examples belong to group 1, one to group 2 and two to group 3.

a *Please let me know as soon as you have fixed your travel plans.*
b *I have just received this from John Merritt.*
c *I'll come home when I have finished work.*
d *I have lived here all my life.*
e *I haven't booked my ticket yet.*

---

196 ## English sounds

196a **a** What sound do these words have in common?

useful, you, Europe, yes, yet, unusual, future, years

196b **b** **Going to** used to refer to the future is so common that it is often pronounced /gənə/.

What are you going to see?
Are you going to do this thing alone?
Are you going to play tennis?

---

197 # Picture story

Work in groups and see if you can make up a story from these pictures. Tell your story to the class.

81

198 Other people's stories

a Here are two more stories about the pictures in section 197.

Which story is more like yours, the first or the second?

1
> A man was walking down the street when he passed a woman carrying a suitcase. Suddenly he realised it was someone he knew, so he called out and ran after her. She was afraid as she didn't recognise the man. She dropped the case and ran away as fast as she could. The man stopped and picked up the case and opened it, but there was nothing inside, no clue to her identity.
>
> R W

2
> Mr. Smith had lost his suitcase and was looking everywhere for it. He walked along the street and noticed a woman walking in the other direction carrying his suitcase. "Hey, that's mine," he shouted. "Give it back." The woman, thinking the man was really angry, dropped the suitcase and ran as fast as she could. Mr. Smith carried his suitcase home, opened it up and discovered it was full of women's clothes
>
> E F

b Which of these experiences have you had?

Have you ever lost anything like a suitcase?
Have you ever spoken to someone you thought you knew, and then realised that it wasn't the person you thought it was?

Have you ever taken something belonging to someone else by mistake? (Picked up the wrong bag of shopping, for example?)
Have you ever seen a thief taking something from someone?

What would you say in each of these situations?

c Now look at the pictures in section 197 again and write a story of your own. Write it using the past tense.
If you want to change the order of the pictures this time, you can.

199 A warning

Charlie, I'm warning you about your hours. The night before last you came home yesterday. Last night you came home today. This evening, if you come home tomorrow, I won't be here.

200 Grammar words

so

1 marking a summary or a change of subject
A: *I wasn't in London last weekend.* B: *So, you weren't in London last weekend?*
BG: *I haven't really got anything else planned.* DF: *So what about the shopping?*

2 expressing amount
We were so tired that we went straight to bed.

3 meaning 'therefore'
He saw someone he thought he knew, so he called out and ran after her.

4 pointing back
A: *It's very easy.* B: *Do you really think so?*

5 **so that** used to talk about result or purpose
The British Council helps British participants by helping to pay their expenses so that they can attend the Seminar.

6 meaning 'also'
A: *I've got some money.* B: *So have I.*

___

There is one example below of each of these six meanings of **so**. Which is which?

a DF: *Will you be going to Nisa this weekend?* BG: *Yes, I think so.* DF: *So will I. So that's one possibility.*
b A: *It depends if I've got a car or not.* B: *Right, so you do your shopping by car.*
c *Please let me know as soon as you have fixed your travel plans so that I can make sure you are properly looked after on arrival.*
d *After so much hassle I'm determined to stay at the top.*

201 Arranging to meet

201 George and Mary are trying to arrange to meet sometime next week. Can you fill in the blanks in their conversation?

M: *George? This is Mary.*
G: *Hi. Good to hear you.*
M: *Look, can we meet some time next week? ___ ___ Monday morning?*
G: *Monday morning? No. I'm sorry _____ _____ to be in Paris then. I don't get back _____ Wednesday.*
M: *Oh dear. Wednesday's no good for me. _____ _____ all day Wednesday.*
G: *Thursday? How about Thursday?*
M: *Thursday morning?*
G: *Well, _____ _____ on Thursday morning. _____ _____ the afternoon?*
M: *No. _____ _____ to Manchester on Thursday afternoon. _____ _____ to be Friday afternoon.*
G: *Okay, what time?*
M: *Two thirty?*
G: *_____. See you two thirty on Friday. Okay?*
M: *_____. Fine.*

202 *Grammar words*

been

1 used to make the present perfect of **go**
North America, yes. I haven't been there, but it looks very much like the photographs that you see.
You've been to South America haven't you?

2 used to make the present perfect with **-ing**
I've been learning English for more than a year.
We haven't been living here long.

3 used to make the present perfect of **be**
How long have you been there?
I have not been able to finalise my arrangements yet.

4 used to make the present and past perfect passive (with **-ed**)
Some windmills have been converted into houses.
It has often been said that the British talk a lot about the weather.

What categories do these examples belong to?

a *I've never been to Spain.*
b *Many beautiful trees and flowers have been brought to Kew Gardens.*
c *There has been a lot of rain this week.*
d *I've been waiting here for half an hour.*

203 Short notes

```
PLEASE INFORM DR TICKOO, RELC, HAVE NOW SENT LETTER AND
COPY OF SEMINAR PAPER.  APOLOGIES FOR DELAY.
```

a Can you put these words into the telex to make a full version of the message?

a, at, I, I, give him, my, on, please, that, the, the, the

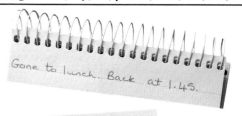

Gone to lunch. Back at 1.45.

Date and time for meeting not yet fixed.
Probably 14.00 Thursday.

b Can you rewrite these short notes in full?

Have you and your partner got the same messages?

Sorry. Won't be in for supper.

Back at midnight. Key in usual place.

9.30. Couldn't wait any longer. See you next week.

Back about 9. Please keep supper warm.

c Do you ever have to leave messages? Do you ever write telexes or notes for people? What notes might you write to members of your family, or friends, or people at work?

▷ Write three messages in note form. Give them to someone else. Can they tell what you mean? Can they write them out in full? Can they write you an answer?

83

a Expressing the future

Find these words in the examples below.

> as soon as possible, at some stage, come, future, going, intend, look forward, plan, see, shall, should, will, won't, would

If you come home tomorrow I won't be there.
The British Council will contribute £500.
Will your paths cross?
I shall be staying with Vijay Bhatia. I shall let you know as soon as I have heard from him.
I shall have to confirm these timings.
I'll see what happens.
They're going on holiday.
Are you going to play tennis?
What four questions would you ask?
I should arrive in Singapore at 13.50.
I'm planning to come to Singapore.
I intend to come to Singapore.
I look forward to seeing you in April.
What does Bridget say about her future?
What about your future plans?
I have not yet got confirmation so I shall have to confirm as soon as possible.
I'll have to go shopping at some stage.

b ????

What word can you use to complete all of these sentences?

How about this picture the big vase?
Yes. I think I agree you.
Is it anything to do sport?
Is it something to do your family?
Are you going to have dinner out friends?
I'm going to have lunch the family.
I help John out all his administration.
Farmers do a lot of work a combine harvester.
Very best wishes, yours sincerely, . . .

c above, afraid, book, both . . . and, concerned with, to do with, inside, quite, yet

Notice how these words and phrases are used. Which two are similar in meaning?

I am writing with regard to my travelling arrangements for the above seminar.
She was afraid as she didn't recognise the man.
I haven't booked my ticket yet.
With warmest regards to both you and Jane.
Is it concerned with music?
Is it something to do with sport?
Is it a game you play inside a room?
No, you don't play it inside.
So you're quite happy with it?

---

42 Game (see Unit 3)

Important words to remember (668 so far)

above	arrive	future	should	understand
again	been	lose	soon	whether
arrangement	below	receive	therefore	

205 ## Instructions

a How do you use these different types of payphones? Which photo is which?

b What would you do in an emergency? Look at this page from a British phone book and put the instructions in the right order.

All you need to know here
How to telephone: Most red street kiosks (yellow in some places) take 10p coins only, but many city centres, main railway stations and airports have new blue payphones which accept all UK coins (except 1p).
With these new phones you must put in the money before making your call. In some areas you will find green cardphones which use small plastic credit cards costing between £1.00 and £20.00. These are available in post offices, news stands, bars and shops. Whatever system you use, read the instructions on the back wall first, and remember that when dialling a number from within the same area you do not need the prefix. For instance, in London

999
emergencies

Fire

Police

Ambulance

Cave Rescue

Coastguard
(sea and cliff rescue)

Mountain Rescue

Give the address where help is needed

Wait for the emergency service to answer

Dial 999 or the emergency number shown on the number label

Give any other necessary information

Give the telephone number shown on the phone

Tell the operator which service you want

Dialling 999 is free
To dial in darkness or in smoke, it will help if you know where the hole or button is on your phone. Remembering where it is and practising finding it with your eyes closed could make an enormous difference in a real emergency.

Other Emergency Services
For other emergencies, eg
Gas ■ Water ■ Electricity
see ALPHABETICAL LISTINGS

Samaritans
01-283 3400

c How do telephones in your country compare with those in Britain? What different types do you have? Can you make international phone calls from any public phone box?

206 Telephoning home

a Look at the brochure extract on the right. Which system is quicker, direct dialling or calling via the operator? Which is cheaper?

206b **b** Pips, bleeps or 'burr-burr'? Read the British Telecom information below, and say which sounds you hear.

TONES

The British Telephone system uses tones which differ in some respects from those in other countries.

Dial tone
A continuous purring or high-pitched hum.

Ringing tone
A repeated 'burr-burr' sound.

Engaged (busy) tone
A repeated single note.

Number unobtainable
A continuous steady note. This means that the number is out of order, or currently not in use, or an incorrect dialling code has been used.

Pay tone
(Used in the older style pay-on-answer payphones.) A rapid series of short pips. You should insert money while this tone is sounding.

WELCOME TO BRITAIN: how to telephone home

British Telecom International would like to welcome you to Britain and hopes you will enjoy your stay.

While you are here you may wish to contact friends and relations at home to find out how they are getting on without you and tell them what you have seen and done in the UK.

What better way than by telephone? You can telephone to almost anywhere in the world from the UK, but it's quicker, cheaper and easier when you can dial direct, especially from a British Telecom payphone. This booklet's aim is to help you.

c Match each instruction on the left with one which means the same on the right.

Put the money in.	Key the number.
Check the credit display.	Lift the handset.
Lift the receiver.	Insert coins.
Dial the number.	Look at the reading to see how much money there is left.

206d **d** Look at the three types of telephone below. Which of these three types of telephone did Danny and Bridget discuss the instructions for, and in what order? Which one do you think would be easiest to use?

▶ 206d Make clear notes of Danny and Bridget's instructions.

TYPES OF PAYPHONE

Press-button payphones
There are now several types of modern payphones with press-button dialling to be found in busy centres and most tourist areas. They are the most suitable for making international calls and can be divided into two sorts, coin-operated payphones and cardphones.

1 Coin-operated payphones
There are two types. One takes 2p, 10p, and 50p coins and the other 2p, 5p, 10p, 20p, 50p and £1 coins. Calls may be dialled direct to anywhere in the UK and to all the countries to which International Direct Dialling is available.

2 Cardphones
These are quickly becoming more widely available. To use these phones you must first buy one of the special cards which are available from Post Offices and shops displaying the green 'Cardphone' sign. You may then make any number of calls up to the value of the card, whenever you wish, without the need for cash. You may find them more convenient for phoning home than ordinary payphones, especially if you intend to make several calls during your stay. Please note, you cannot use Cardphones for calls via the operator.

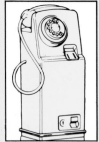

'Pay-on-answer' payphones
These are the older types of payphones, but they are still fairly widespread. They take 10p coins and calls may be made to anywhere in the UK, Europe, parts of North Africa, North America, and the Caribbean. However, because the time allowed for 10p on international calls is limited, these payphones are more suitable for inland calls.

e Describe how to telephone the USA or the UK from your country. Prepare a set of instructions for one type of telephone that is common. Write them out clearly.

Explain to the class what types of payphone you have in your country, and how to make a call abroad.

How many different types of payphone do you know of between you?

a Instructions: spoken and written

Find a written instruction in section 206c which means the same as the spoken instructions in colour below.

BG: Well, which – we're going to do the press-button one first. [...]
DL: Yeah.
BG: Okay. Well you lift the receiver first.
DL: Yes.
BG: Then you put in your money.
DL: Yes.
BG: Then you dial the number you want.
DL: Correct.
BG: And then if you get through your money falls into the machine, and if you don't get through and don't speak to anybody you get your money back.

DL: But, when you put your money in, there is a little, erm, reading that shows up how much money you've put in.
BG: Yes.

DL: And, the money I think has actually already gone into the machine. So, if you don't get through, then you hang up again, and the money will then fall out.
It won't – you can't – I don't think you can redial straight away, can you?

BG: Some of them have a button that you press, and without having to take your – let your money come out and put it in again you can redial.

DL: Now we go on to the dial phone.
Well, er, again we – one lifts the receiver. Only this time instead of putting your money in first, you dial the number that you require, and you hear a ringing tone. Once the person has – that you're trying to contact, has lifted their phone, at the other end, the ringing tone will stop, and a series of – how would you describe – ?
BG: Pips.
DL: Pips. Bleeps. Erm ... at rather frequent intervals, start. What you hear then down the phone. Erm, and at that point you push your money in. And er, that's it.

What are the main differences between these spoken instructions and the usual written instructions?

b Read the part of the transcript at the top of this column again and find the words **we, one, you, your** and **their**. Who do these words refer to?

Who does the word **they** refer to in each of these examples?

I rang you at your hotel but they said you were out.

A: *Someone rang when you were out.* B: *Oh, who?* A: *I don't know, they didn't give their name.*

c may, must and **need**

Look at the British Telecom brochure in section 206. Can you find five phrases with **may**, one with **must**, and one with **need**? Write them down.

What would you do if...?

Discuss briefly what you would do if you were in one of these situations.

- if you heard the fire alarm in the building you are in now
- if the electricity went off in your home, and you thought it might be a power cut
- if you were by the sea and you heard someone shouting for help

Together with your partner, plan what you would say. If you were with a friend, what would you tell them to do?

▶ Act out the situation in front of the class. Don't say which of the three situations it is. Can the others guess what has happened?

if

Look at **if** in the Grammar Book.
What categories do these sentences belong to?

a *It will help if you know where the hole or button is in your phone.*
b *If you were counting how would you say these numbers?*
c *Listen to the recording and see if you were right.*
d *They tried to find out if their paths would cross.*
e *It sounds as if it's engaged.*
f *What would you do if you heard the fire alarm?*

210 Stories

210a a WRONG NUMBER?

Eagerly I answered the telephone and heard a male voice ask, 'Is Rosemary there?'
'I'm sorry,' I said. 'You must have got the wrong number.'
There was a pause, then the caller said tentatively, 'Elaine?' I confirmed that this was my name.
There was another awkward silence, then he said, 'Oh, you were next on my list.'

How do you think Elaine felt at the beginning? What about at the end?

b This is the first part of a story. Discuss what you think had happened to the woman on the other end of the telephone.

END OF CONVERSATION

An obviously distressed woman phoned the local police and said she had been talking to a friend on the telephone when the conversation ceased and she heard gasping sounds . . .

210b Now listen to the sounds on tape and see if you can work out the rest of the story.

Finally read the rest of the story at the bottom of this page and see if you were right.

c Mystery play

210c Tell your partner what you think happened. Do you agree?
What is the connection between this play and the following piece of advice?

A HELPFUL HINT

> For extra light during a power cut, put a candle and holder in a large shallow dish filled with water, and place in front of a mirror. The water and the mirror will reflect the light and make things brighter.

211 *Language study*

Past tense verb forms

All these common verbs are used in section 210. Read through the stories quickly and check that you know what their past tense forms are.

> answer, hear, say, is, are, feel, phone, has, give, look, see, try, come, explain

212 Puzzle

INTERNATIONAL TIME

Gill lives in London, but has a good friend in San Francisco. They occasionally ring each other up.
Gill's friend is out at work all day, usually from 8 a.m. to 5.45 p.m., and she also goes out quite a lot in the evenings. There is 8 hours' time difference between the two countries in the winter, London being ahead of San Francisco.

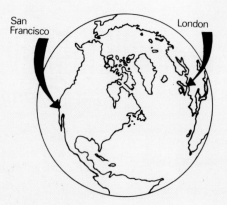

What time would be best for Gill to phone her friend?

> Write down the time you decide on, and your reason for choosing it.

Do other people in your class agree with your choice?

212 What time did David and Bridget think would be the most sensible, and why?

Continuation of story (210b)

A constable rushed to the address she gave. He knocked at the door and got no response. He looked in through the window and saw a woman lying on the floor beside the telephone.

Before attempting to break down the door, the man tried knocking again, and to his surprise the victim rose and came to the door. She explained that her friend had been talking to her for more than an hour, and that she had simply fallen asleep.

Grammar words

-ing

1 describing something
There were two girls eating fish and chips.
Write down one or two interesting things about each person.

2 after **am, is, be** etc.
One girl was carrying a white bag.
The S student will be asking you questions about things that you usually do during the day.

3 after **see, look at, hear, listen to** etc.
Listen to them talking about when they go to bed.

4 before **am, is** etc.
Dialling 999 is free.

5 after **stop, start, remember, like** etc.
I remember going to London many years ago.
She likes watching television.

6 after **when, before, instead of** etc.
Remember that when dialling a number from within the same area, you do not need the prefix.
Before attempting to break down the door, the man tried …

Write down five of these things.

> something you like doing
> something you stopped doing a long time ago
> something you can see someone doing
> what you were doing at this time yesterday
> what you will be doing this time tomorrow
> something you remember doing as a child
> someone who is sitting at the front of the class

What categories do these sentences belong to?

a *Put in the money before making your call.*
b *Listen to David and Bridget discussing the same problem.*
c *The conversation ceased and she heard gasping sounds.*
d *Using a cardphone is not difficult.*
e *You can telephone your family back home without using money.*
f *The special cards are available from Post Offices and shops displaying the green 'Cardphone' sign.*
g *I really like running. Swimming is nice too.*
h *You have quite a long working day, don't you?*

English sounds

214 Which sound does each set have in common?

1 put in, hang up, speak to, pips, 8p, pretty modern, help, public, private, payphone

2 if you …, telephone, left with 2p, 2.15, lift, ladies first! call for help, fire, photograph

215

Record a message

Telephone answering machines are getting more and more common these days.

> Hello, Fred here. Oh…erm, er, okay, it's Fred here. It's about the party next weekend I wanted. to ask you if…

215 Imagine that you had telephoned a friend who was out. Their telephone answering machine asked you to leave a message.

> Now think of a message that you might have either for a friend or for a business colleague.

> There are some ideas here. You would have to start off by giving your name, and the subject of your message.

> *party on ____day*
> *meeting on _____*
> *your invitation to dinner*
> *that film you asked me about*

> *can't come as planned*
> *can I bring a friend?*
> *going to be late*
> *made a mistake about the time of _____*

> *haven't been very well*
> *have to go and see _____*
> *friends have arrived unexpectedly*
> *could you possibly _____*

Exchange messages. Plan an answer to someone else's message.

216 Instructions and warnings

a Look at these photos of some common things that you might find in any house. Find:

something you can eat.
something to drink.
something you can take if you are ill.
something to wash your hair with.
something else that you might use in the bathroom.
something to stop mosquitoes biting you.

b Parts of these labels are missing. Can you find a suitable label for each item?

For fastest knockdown action, spray directly at the insect. For complete protection spray into the room for a few seconds, keeping the doors and windows closed.

DO NOT SPRAY DIRECTLY ON FOOD.

DANGEROUS TO FISH – remove fish bowls before spraying.

KEEP IN A SAFE PLACE AWAY FROM YOUNG CHILDREN.

ADULTS – One or two 5 ml spoonfuls every two or three hours.
CHILDREN – 1 to 5 years: Half a 5 ml spoonful every three or four hours. 6 to 12 years: One 5 ml spoonful every three or four hours.

JUNGLE FORMULA
Repels mosquitoes, midges and most biting flies for up to 8 hours.
CARE
Do not use on acetate, rayon or synthetic plastic finishes – keep away from plastic and varnished surfaces. Avoid contact with heat and fire.
DIRECTIONS FOR USE
Apply to all exposed skin except lips and eyes. Re-seal container securely after use.
Pack and contents produced in the U.K. for:
THE JUNGLE FORMULA COMPANY, PULBOROUGH, WEST SUSSEX.

Hold the can about 12 inches from your hair and spray lightly and evenly. Avoid spraying near eyes. **CAUTION: FLAMMABLE. DO NOT USE NEAR FIRE OR FLAME. Keep out of the reach of children.**

Once opened keep refrigerated & eat within 3 days.

To use: Wet hair. Lather. Rinse. Repeat.

KEEP FIRMLY CLOSED

1 tablet to be taken 3 times daily after food.

217 *Language study*

Directions and warnings

a Some of these instructions tell you how to use the product (directions for use). Others tell you how not to use it.

Read the labels again, and find words and phrases which warn you about possible dangers. Write them down so that you won't forget them.
For example: *Avoid* ...

b Words ending in -ly

What do these words ending in **-ly** tell us about?

directly	
lightly	how to ...
evenly	when to ...
daily	how not to ...
firmly	where to ...
centrally	

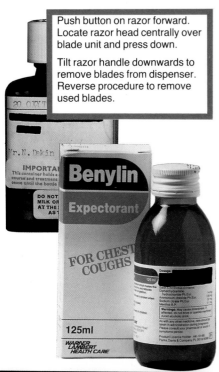

Push button on razor forward. Locate razor head centrally over blade unit and press down.

Tilt razor handle downwards to remove blades from dispenser. Reverse procedure to remove used blades.

Benylin Expectorant

FOR CHEST COUGHS

125ml

WARNER LAMBERT HEALTH CARE

Avoid high temperature & strong light.
C. SHIPPAM LTD. CHICHESTER, WEST SUSSEX
MADE IN ENGLAND
NUTRITI PER 35g

SHIPPAMS Beef PASTE

For external use only – keep out of reach of children. Avoid contact with lips and eyes.

Wordpower

keep

1 make something or somebody stay in a particular position or state

to keep the food hot

2 have something and not throw it away, give it to someone else or lose it

Keep those notes. They might be useful.

3 put something in a particular place and store it there

You should either keep your Driving Licence with you, or keep it in the car.

4 repeatedly do a particular action

I kept making the same mistake.

Listen. It keeps making a funny noise!

Look at the examples here. There are three belonging to category 1, two to category 2, one to category 3, and three to category 4.

A: *Can we keep these, please, or must we give them back?*

B: *No, they're for you to keep.*

Close the windows. It'll keep the room warmer.

Now look at the labels in section 216. Find six more examples of **keep**. Which categories do they belong to?

Giving advice; making complaints

219 Read the dialogues and practise saying them after the tape.

A: *Just look at this – I only bought it last week.*

B: *That's awful. You should take it back to the shop. You really should.*

A: *Oh, I couldn't do that.*

B: *Well, I would, if I were you. Take it back, ask for the manager, and ask for your money back.*

A: *Oh, all right, I will, then.*

C: *Sorry to keep you waiting. Can I help you?*

A: *Yes, I bought this here a week ago and look what's happened.*

C: *Oh dear, yes. Mm. Right. Could I possibly see your receipt?*

A: *My receipt? But I haven't kept the receipt.*

C: *Oh, well, I'm very sorry, very sorry indeed, but we can't change anything without the receipt . . .*

Think of a situation you might be in yourself, and make up a similar dialogue. Act it out for your friends to watch.

a Necessary or not necessary?

...ve to ...st ...ssary to ...e work unless you ...d to	put the money in first.

Give any other necessary information.
Give any other information that is needed.
Give the address where help is needed.

You	don't have to pay. don't need to pay.
There's no need to pay.	

A: *What money do I need?* B: *You need 15p in change. You must have the right change.*

b Getting people to do things

		Give the telephone number ...
	You	give the telephone number ...
Could	you	give the telephone number?

Make more sentences like these from the table on the right. Put capital letters where necessary.

	you	go and get help. check the power supply. press the button. take it back to the shop. close all the doors. call the fire service. get off the bus past the hospital. turn the lights off.
could can will would	you	

c ????

Which word fits all the spaces? (Sometimes it needs an **s** on the end.)

1.1 to do part of a job for someone
A: *Shall I _____ you clean the car?* B: *No thanks, but you could _____ me with this box.*

1.2 to give advice
A: *Can I _____ you?*
B: *Please. Where can I get a ...?*

1.3
Oxfam gives _____ to Third World countries – food and money.

2
It _____ if you read the instructions first!
It will _____ if you know how to use the telephone in darkness.
Write three words to _____ you remember.

3
Thanks very much. You've been a great _____.

4
_____! Can you go for _____?

5
Whoops! Sorry! But I couldn't _____ it!

d may

1 *You may want to phone home.* (= perhaps, you might want to)
2 *You may make any number of calls.* (= you can, it's possible to)
3 *May I come in?* (= Can/Could I come in please? – asking permission to)

e it

Look at the Grammar Book. Which category does each set of examples of **it** best go into?

Whoops! Sorry! But I couldn't help it.
Phone her at 3.30. That would be more sensible, wouldn't it?
You push your money in and that's it.

It's 10.30. Yes. It's time to go home.
It's lovely weather, isn't it?

Let your money come out, then put it in again.
The phone rang, so he answered it.
Where's my book? Oh, I've seen it somewhere. It's over there!

It's quicker, cheaper and easier to dial direct.
It's so hard not to forget something.

f should

... normal telephone service is not available and no money should be inserted.
Find out what you should do in case of fire in your building.
What should you do when telephoning in an emergency?
Which order should the instructions go in?

Important words to remember (689 so far)

available	fire	if	necessary	service	whatever
daily	free	instruction	power	situation	while
emergency	hear	keep	private	speak	within
especially	help	machine	public	telephone	

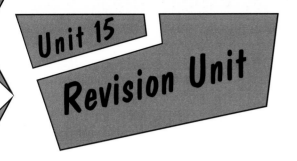

Myf's son Fergus in Monze, Zambia

221 Myf's travel plans

What experience do you and your family have of Africa? Have you ever seen any films about Africa? Have you read anything about Africa? Has anyone in your family ever lived there, or been there? If so, which part? Tell each other.

Look at this section and write down four things you think Myf will be doing on her trip to Zambia. Who might she be with? How do you think she'll be travelling?

REPUBLIC OF
Zambia

Zambia the real Africa

South Luangwa National Park

Kafue Game Park

Zambezi River

Lusaka

The International Game Park

Lake Kariba

Victoria Falls

Zambia: *Zambia's Victoria Falls – one of the world's Seven Wonders*

BARGAIN FLIGHTS
EUROPE/WORLDWIDE
TEL: 01-323 4941
CANARIES

South Luangwa National Park is about 737 kilometres from Lusaka and located in the North East of Zambia. Zambia Airways flies to the park four times a week on a 75-minute flight by HS748 from Lusaka International Airport.

Kafue National Park is 22,500 square kilometres in extent – the size of Wales or half that of Switzerland – it lies about 330 kilometres west of Lusaka and is one of the largest game sanctuaries in Africa.

Zambia: *Topless four-wheel safari*

Tell each other what you think Myf's plans are, and put all your ideas together. Write a list of the things you think she'll be doing.

221 Myf talks to Bob Bushaway about her plans. How many of her plans did you guess correctly?

222 Is it true that...?

Mark these sentences T for *true*, NT for *not true* or ? for *don't know*.

a *Myf has bought her ticket for Zambia already.*
b *She has planned to meet her son in Lusaka.*
c *She'll be setting off in September.*
d *She will be staying in Africa for six months.*
e *She has never been to Zambia before.*
f *Her son has been working there with VSO.*
g *He has already been in Zambia for almost a year.*
h *They're going to go on safari.*
i *Zambia's game parks have become quite famous recently.*
j *They may go down to the Victoria Falls and on to Zimbabwe too.*
k *The flight to Lusaka is a direct flight and it will take around twelve hours.*

93

223 Language study

a Referring to the future

221 Find all the phrases that refer to Myf's future plans. How many ways are there of referring to the future?

BB: Right Myf, I hear you're er, planning a trip to Africa.
MS: Yes. It's very exciting. Going in er, September to see my son who's er – he's doing VSO in Af- – in Zambia. So, I'm going to fly to, erm . . . Lusaka, and, erm, he'll meet me there. And we'll do a bit of travelling round. I think we're going to be staying most of the time in Monze, which is where he's working. It's about er, erm . . . a hundred yard- – miles south of er, Lusaka. But we're planning all sorts of exciting things. We're going to go on safari –
BB: How long are you actually going for?
MS: Oh, erm . . . six weeks. Quite a – quite a long time so we can do quite a lot. Er . . . going to saf- – erm . . . think we're going to one of the big game parks – Luangwa – a game park, for a few days.
BB: Right.

MS: Erm . . . Probably going on down to see the Victoria Falls. And we're going – actually going to Zimbabwe as well. Erm . . .
BB: And what – ?
MS: And that –
BB: Matter of interest. What airline are you planning to fly by?
MS: Sorry? Er . . . Air Zambia.
BB: Air Zambia.

b of

Write down the phrases in the transcript with the word **of**. (There are six. Myf uses five, and Bob just one.) For example:

we'll do a bit of travelling around.

There are also at least eight phrases with **of** in section 221. Can you find them? Write them down too. Look at the Grammar Book and see which categories they fit into.

224 Your travel plans

Write a short list of any plans you have for a future trip. If you have no plans at all, write about somewhere you might like to go at some point in the future.

Prepare to interview three other people about their plans. You are going to fill in a table like the one on the right. What questions might be useful? Write some down. For example:

Are you going by car or train or what?
or *How are you travelling?*

▶ Find three people to ask about their plans. Fill in the table. ◀

Name:			
Where			
Who with			
How			
When			
How long for			
What kind of things to do			

Write a short report on what you found out. Don't mention any names. For example:

Two people are planning to go away in July. One of them is going to stay with . . . The other is . . .

Let other people read your report and find out if any of them interviewed the same people, or whether any other people in the class have similar plans.

225 Not such a busy day

Friday was Shirley Williams' last working day of the week after her business trip to South America. She had had no time off the weekend before, because she had been travelling back to the UK. So that weekend she intended to meet her daughter Becky and take things easy. Two things, however, did not turn out as she had expected. Can you guess what they were?

Read about what happened on Friday and find out what these two things were. Was she happy or unhappy about them? Say why.

		🚆	🚆
London Euston	d	14 05	14 30
Kensington Olympia	d	—	
Watford Junction	d	—	
Stafford	a	—	16 15	16
Stoke-on-Trent	a	—	17 15b	17
Crewe	a	16 14	16 44

Mondays to Fridays *continued*

RadioTimes

10.5 Question Time

Among **Sir Robin Day's** guests tonight at the Greenwood Theatre, London, for the last programme in the present series are **James Cooke, Ken Livingstone** and **The Rt Hon Shirley Williams.**

FRIDAY

I was up at 7.45, had a boiled egg and went back to the German Embassy for further meetings. Friday was a relatively quiet day and I had a social weekend planned.

I needed it after the previous hectic week. I had lunch with some friends and then caught the train to Crewe to meet my daughter. People talked to me all the time on the train, asking me what I thought about 'Question Time'. I had intended to do some work, but I didn't really get the chance. I like to speak to people, anyway, because I get to know their views and what worries them.

My daughter was an hour late, so I stood glumly on the station being pointed and stared at; I find it really embarrassing when people do that. When Becky arrived we drove up to the Lake District and booked into a guest house.

Language study

a Common phrases

Find words to finish these phrases from the text 'Friday' in section 225.

*for further . . .
a social . . .
People talked to me all the . . .
I had intended to do some . . .
but I didn't really get the . . .
I like to speak to people . . .
because I get to know their . . .
My daughter was an hour . . .
being pointed and stared . . .
I find it really . . .
and booked into a guest . . .*

Learn some of the phrases.

b Common question forms

These are questions that either Shirley Williams or her daughter might have asked when they met at Crewe Station. Can you finish each question using words from the right, and then say which person might have asked them?

Where were you at	*arrive?*
What time did you	*last night?*
When did you get back from	*4.44?*
Why didn't you come up	*talk to on the train?*
Who did you	*South America?*

227 Make up a story

Can you make up a story to fit these pictures? You can put them in any order you like.

Write some notes to help you tell your story.

Read out your story and see if people can say what order the pictures are in.

228 Interviews

Divide into two groups. Look back at sections 163 and 225.

Prepare to interview someone in the other group about a day in the last week so that you can write a similar report.

Read each other's reports.

229 Household objects

229a a Danny had a list of household objects and had to choose one.
Bridget tried to guess the object he had chosen.

Listen for the answers to these questions.

Is it large?
Is it used for something?
Has it got legs?
Do people use it?
Do you find them in a house or outside?
Could you find it in any room in the house?

b Bridget finds out that it's plugged in, that it's in the kitchen, that you don't have to touch it to use it and that you don't have to move it around.

It's in the picture below. What is it?

c Find these things in the picture.

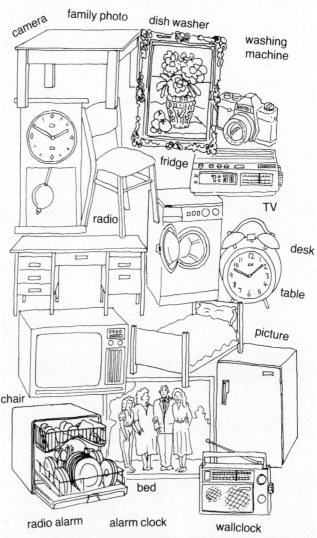

Choose one of these things and play the same game.

230 Other people's stories

230a **a** An American called Ted made up a story to fit the pictures in section 227. This is what he wrote.

In some places you have to decide which word Ted used.

What order did Ted put the pictures in?

Jup | arrives / gets | home from school, | makes / gets | himself something to eat, and | finally / then | sits down to do his homework. 'Oh dear! A test tomorrow, and I've forgotten my book. Aminah has her book, | I know / I'm sure |, but it's such a long | way / walk | to her | house / place |. Oh well. It must be done, I | guess / suppose | ...'

'Aminah, hi! | Could / Can | I borrow your book to | study / prepare | for the test tomorrow?'

'Sure, I won't be needing it.'

('Hmm, I wonder why she won't be needing it. Isn't she | studying / preparing | for the test? Why did she smile and wink when I | wanted / asked | to borrow her book?')

All night long Jup | studies / reads | the book. Morning | comes / arrives | and Jup goes to his classroom. 'There's no test today. It's next week!' says Aminah.

'She knew | all along / all the time |,' thinks Jup ...

---

b The authors' daughter wrote a story as well. Her story was much shorter than Ted's.

A man had just come home from a walk up a hill when he realised that he had left his book in the café at the top of the hill. He climbed all the way back up the hill to get it, and he found his sister, who he hadn't seen for years, in the café.

---

232 Stories

a What words are missing from the end of this story?

Lovely day, isn't it?
Jogging for the first time in my new neighbourhood, I saw another solitary figure running towards me. 'Lovely day, isn't it?' I called out. We passed before he could reply. The next day, I set out again, and saw the same runner heading towards me. As we quickly passed, he shouted back, '_____ _____ _____!'

232a See what the last words were.

---

231 Language study

had

a These sentences tell the events in the second story in the order they happened.

1 A man left his book in the café at the top of the hill.
2 He came home from his walk.
3 He realised 1.
4 He climbed back up the hill to get his book.
5 He found his sister in the cafe.

Look at this version.

(4) *Joe was climbing back up a steep hill.* (2) *He had just come home from a long walk and* (3) *had realised* (1) *he had left his book in a café at the top of the hill.* (5) *When he finally got to the café he was surprised to find his sister there.*

What has happened to sentences 1, 2 and 3?

b Why are only some verbs formed with **had** in these examples?

Shirley Williams had had *no time off the weekend before, because she* had been travelling *back to the UK from South America. So this weekend she* intended ... *to take things easy.*

Ruth and Claire had been *friends since the age of three. In 1978 Ruth* moved away ...

An obviously distressed woman phoned the local police and said *she* had been talking *to a friend.*

She explained *that her friend* had been talking *to her for more than an hour and she* had simply fallen *asleep.*

His suitcase had been lost *and he* was looking *for it.*

---

c Most of the verbs in Ted's story are in the present tense. Do they refer to the present?

▷ Tell the second story in the present tense. ◁

▷ **d** Can you write a very short summary of Ted's story in the past tense? ◁

---

b This story happens in America. Read it and guess what word is missing.

Ninety-seven today
My 81-year-old mother is proud of the fact that she doesn't look her age. One summer day she went into a drugstore and, talking about the heat, said to the clerk, 'Going to be ninety-seven today.'
The man reached across the counter, shook her hand and said, 'Happy _____.' Mother took to her bed for a week.

97° fahrenheit = 36° Celsius

232b Listen and find out.

233 Letter from a seven-year-old

Ruth and Claire had been very close friends since the age of three, when they went to nursery school together. In 1978, Ruth moved away, so they started writing to each other.
At the end of June 1979, Claire wrote to Ruth, asking her to come and stay for three days during the school holidays. She also told Ruth what she had been doing recently.

Read Ruth's reply, and try to work out what three main things Claire must have written about in her letter to Ruth.

Can you find the following words in Ruth's letter?

> didn't, forward, friends, from, haven't, holidays, missed

Why do you think Ruth spelt these words as she did?

Find the phrases **look forward** and **on your letter**. There is one thing wrong with each phrase as it is used in the letter. What would be more correct here?

Claire and Ruth, aged 4

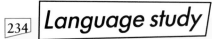

1979 Monday July 16th   37 Northdene
                               Limesfarm estate
                               Chigwell Essex

dear claire
    I hope you are well I am well I am look
Ford to seeing you for 3 days in the summer
holdays and I haven't been to any circus or
zoos fairs and I did'en know what you were
talking About when You Said on your letter
Something about a horse race and I have
been to Swansea and been to see the Seaside
and my freands Live there called Eiwen and Kiersti
and Susan and damian and their daddy
and mommy are called gail and bob Allen and
we mist a day at school that was Monday
and I had a nice time there
      Love frome
        Ruth xxxxx

234 *Language study*

a How many full stops did Ruth use? How did she divide her letter into 'sentences'?

b What other things in Ruth's letter tell you that it was written by a child (apart from her handwriting, of course!)?

If an older child had wanted to give the same information, how might they have written it? Can you write this letter as if from an older child?

235 *Grammar words*

the

The main use of **the** is to say to the listener or reader 'You know which one I mean'. Look at the story in section 232b.

> the heat   = the heat of the day
> the clerk = the clerk in the drugstore
> the man   = the clerk
> the counter = the counter in the drugstore

Sometimes we say which one we mean.

The fact that she doesn't look her age.

1 you know which one the speaker or writer means because they tell you which one, there is only one, or there is only one around
The woman in my picture is carrying a pink bag.
the sun   the kitchen
the world   the queen

2 instead of a possessive like **my, his, her, their** etc.
I have left my book in the house.

3 referring to a whole group of people or things
The Romans grew grapes in Britain.
The young should care for the old.

Which category does each of these examples belong to?

a *Would you close the door please?*
b *Dad, can I borrow the car please?*
c *Oxfam gets money to buy food for the poor.*
d *Neil Armstrong was the first man on the moon.*
e *Write your name on the board.*
f *I felt someone touch me on the arm.*
g *The smallest house in Britain is a fisherman's cottage in Wales.*

97

a Find the word!

How many examples of each of these words can you find?
Do the examples of each word mean the same thing each time?

> actually, air, all, bring/brought, certainly, fact, hope, in, instead, old, part, sure, time, way

MS: *We're going – actually going to Zimbabwe as well.*
BB: *How long are you actually going for?* MS: *Oh, erm . . . six weeks. Quite a – quite a long time.*
BB: *What airline are you planning to fly by?* MS: *Air Zambia.*
I've forgotten to bring my textbook.
Sure, I won't be needing it.
Certainly, I won't be using it.
'She knew all along,' thinks Jup.
Jogging for the first time in my new neighbourhood.
'Lovely day, isn't it?' I called out. He shouted back, 'It certainly is.'
My 81-year-old mother is proud of the fact that she doesn't look her age.
Ruth is an old friend of Claire's.
I hope you are well.

He went all the way back to the café in the hope of finding his book.
He forgot all about his book.
Facts about Britain.
The weather in most parts of Britain will be sunny but cold.
All you need is a phonecard.
Cardphones can be found in airports . . . and in other busy places.
In fact, wherever you see a group of public telephones, you'll usually find that one of them is a cardphone.
I may be able to stop off in Britain on my way to or from the USA in six or eight weeks' time.
I hope by the time you arrive, the weather will have improved.
I hope you have a good time.
You lift the receiver, only this time, instead of putting your money in first, you dial the number . . .

b Past, present or future?

Look again at the examples above, and say whether they refer to past time, present time, or future time.

c since

Ruth and Claire had been close friends since the age of three.
It's such a long time since I saw you last . . .
Two weeks have gone since I started my letter to you.
He had always been a climber ever since he could remember.
Since the beginning of summer it has been hot all the time.
Ruth moved away in 1978 and she and Claire have written to each other ever since.
I've lived here since 1982, ever since I left school in fact.

d ????

come home _____ a walk
got back _____ school
a letter _____ Ruth
It's far away _____ here.
You start _____ here.
Your story is different _____ mine.
apart _____ the handwriting
I stopped him _____ going.
_____ my point of view, . . .

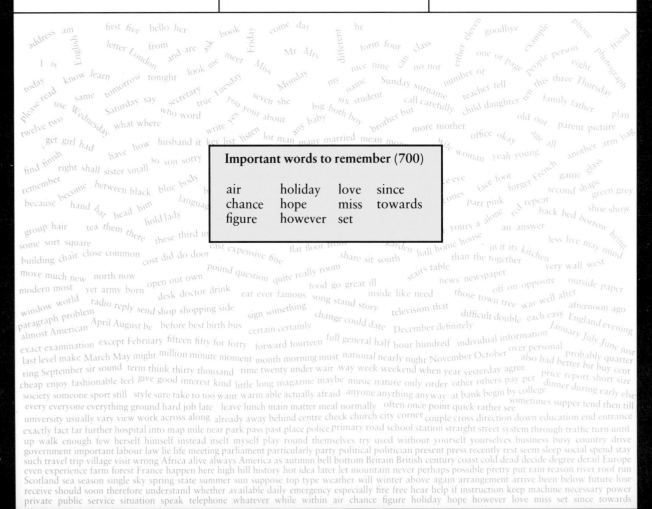

Important words to remember (700)

air	holiday	love	since
chance	hope	miss	towards
figure	however	set	

STUDENT A

38 ## Find the differences

72 ## Find the differences

115 ## A reading puzzle – half a story

John lives with his family in a new block of flats two miles from the town centre. From his flat, they have a nice view of the town.

Every weekday, he leaves his flat at 8.05, and gets in the lift on the 24th floor. He presses the button for the ground floor. He gets out of the lift, says 'Good morning' to the man selling newspapers, goes to the bus stop and gets on a bus.

What floor do you think he lives on?
What floor does he get out of the lift on?

STUDENT B

38 Find the differences

72 Find the differences

115 A reading puzzle – half a story

In the afternoon, John gets a bus about 4.15 and gets back to his block of flats at about 4.45. He usually stops off at the shop to buy some sweets or chocolate, and a newspaper.

He gets in the lift and he presses the button for the 14th floor. At the 14th floor, he gets out, and walks up the stairs to the 24th floor.

If there is someone else in the lift, he gets out at the 24th floor.

What floor do you think he lives on?
Why does he get out at the 14th floor if there is no-one else in the lift?

Grammar Book

List of entries

a, an	get, got	so
as	go	that
at	have, had	the
be	if	to
been	in	wh- words
by	-ing	will, would
can, could	is, are, am, was, were	with
do, did	it	
for	of	

Numbers in brackets after headings refer to sections where you can find more help.
Numbers in brackets after examples show sections where the examples first appear.

a, an (32, 63)

1 not the only one

The man in my picture also has a brown hat. (38)
Do you live in a house or a flat? (52)
The flat is too small for a big family like ours. (107)
Is that a good book? (107)
A: Where do you work? B: Actually I'm a student. (108)

2 how much / many?

She works for a lot of different companies. (24)
Can you open the window a bit, please? (107)
A lot of people are looking for houses in this area. (97)

3 one only

I'll be back in just a moment. (94)
Sit down for a minute and I'll be with you. (94)
A: How far is it? B: About a kilometre.

as (177)

1 'as a . . .', 'as the . . .'

As a child I lived in a small village.
I am speaking to you as a friend.

2 'as . . . as'

She dropped the case and ran away as fast as she could. (198)
Please let me know as soon as you have fixed your travel plans. (193)
Please let me know as soon as possible. (176)

2.1 'same as'

Me too. Same as Bridget. (142)

3 when, while

As you cross Heath Road you will see Woodlands Park. (123)
Chris draws a rough map as Philip talks. (125)
Insert further coins as necessary.

4 'as if'

It also looks to me as if it could be somewhere in Canada, again. (171)
He sounded as if he was very tired.

5 because

She was afraid as she didn't recognise the man. (198)
Bring lots of jumpers as it could be quite cold. (176)

6 'such as'

I would like to stay in a seaside resort, such as Brighton.

7 'as you know'

As you know grapes were grown by the Romans.

8 'as well as'

Remember, work can mean housework or studying as well as doing a job. (110)

at (120)

1 where (which part)

A bedroom at the back. (52)
Where does it come? In the middle or at the end?
What about the one in the middle here at the top? (171)

1.1 in a place where something is happening

I'll phone you at work. (120)
My brother's at Southampton University. (146)
Which were your best subjects at school?
I've got two people sitting at a desk. (72)
What's the best time to phone you at home. (84)

2 when

He says his meeting starts at seven. (76)
I never work at weekends. (109)
I leave the house at about one minute to eight. (118)
At other times she goes to bed after midnight. (113)
At the moment Becky's friend Stephen is staying. (163)

3 'look at', 'shout at', 'stare at' (etc.) someone or something

Look at the numbers on the right. (78)
Bridget and David looked at these pictures in a
  magazine. (96)
I shouted at her to stop her.
He always smiles at me. (120)

4 'at all' (used to emphasise a negative or question)

A: Are you busy? B: Not at all. (120)
And do you have a break at all? (109)

5 used to answer the questions 'how much / old / fast / often' etc.

Oxfam sell things at low prices. (104)
She left school at the age of eighteen.

be

1 after 'will', 'would', 'can', 'could' etc.

I'll be back in just a moment. (94)
Housework can be very hard work.
Which examples would be useful in the classroom?
Bring lots of jumpers as it could be quite cold. (176)
Oriental definitely. It could be Thailand. (171)

2 '... to be' (see to 5)

She aims to be in bed early. (113)
I'll have to be home at nine
Hurry up. We're going to be late.
I don't want to be late.

3 '... be' + -ing

I shall be staying with Vijay Bhatia. (193)

4 'be ...' in advice or an order

Be careful when you cross the road!
Don't be late!
Be quiet!

been (202)

1 used to make the present perfect of 'go' or 'visit'

Have you ever been to Britain?
I've never been outside my own country.

2 used to make the present perfect with -ing

I've been doing it since I was sixteen. (98)
I've been working here in Top Shop for 3 months.
  (98)

3 used to make the present perfect of 'be'

The weather has been rather nice recently.
I have been in touch with the British Council
  Washington. (193)

4 used to make the present and past perfect passive (with -ed / -en)

These pictures have been mixed up.
He got home and found that all his money had been
  taken.

by (111)

1 who / what did it

Wally is awakened by the phone ringing. (91)
Handicrafts made by people in the Third World.
  (104)
Is that a magazine published by Macmillan? (146)

2 how

You solve it by elimination. (158)
English by Radio. (146)
London is only 55 minutes away by train. (179)
Find out by talking to people.

3 when

Everyone helps to clear away after dinner. By then it's
  about 7.15 or 7.30 p.m. (113)
Even though the Forth River is only 66 miles long, by
  the time it reaches Edinburgh it is over 4 miles
  wide. (179)

4 where

Behind the chair? Of the person sitting by the desk?
  (72)
Just by the bus stop. (122)
On the wall by the entrance was a notice. (173)

can, could (93, 138)

1 ability/possibility

What things could you describe as sort of reddish?
  (37)
What other questions could I have asked?
Can you explain the answers? (46)
How much can you remember? (48)
She ran away as fast as she could. (198)
Ten twelve. That could be the time. (78)
Oriental definitely. It could be Thailand. (171)

Make sentences from this frame.

I can .... but I can't ....

Here are some ideas to help you.

> speak English / Italian / Spanish / French / Japanese
> play football / chess / cricket / basketball
> swim / ski / sail a boat / canoe

What can you see?
I couldn't hear what he was saying.

Look at the picture on page 58.
Make three sentences starting:

I can see ...

1.1 'could' for suggestions

You could look in the newspaper.

Make suggestions in answer to these questions.

1 *I want to go out for a good meal. Where could I go?*
2 *I've lost my book. Where could it be?*
3 *The telephone's ringing. Who could it be?*
4 *It's my birthday. What could we do?*

---

2 permission

You can go out now, but come back in ten minutes.
Could I do it tomorrow instead of today?

3 offer / request

Can you give me your address? (11)
Can you spell your name for me? (11)
Can I speak to Dr Brown please? (89)
Can I take a message? (89)
Can you tell me the time, please? (94)
Can you tell me how long it takes?
Could you give me your phone number please? (11)
Could you look after the children for me? (97)

Make six sentences from this table (two offers and four requests).

Can Could	I you	help you tell me the time help me go home early give me a lift carry that for you	(please)?

4   can/could be

That could be John ... but I thought he was at work. (92)

It could be China or Thailand. (171)

Bring lots of jumpers as it can be quite cold. (176)

Imagine you are woken up by a loud noise at night. What could it be?

... the cat? ... a burglar? ... someone coming home late? ... someone in the kitchen? ... someone falling out of bed? ... the neighbours? ... the traffic?

Imagine you are telling someone about it the next day. Say:

It could have been ...

Say which of these things can be:

dangerous / interesting / fun / funny / exciting / boring

| driving fast | TV programmes | parties |
| visiting relatives | travelling by plane | ski-ing |

do, did (132)

1   used to form questions

How many things did he remember? (42)

Where did you live? (57)

Why did you move? (57)

Did you have a look at the shops?

Where did you go yesterday?

Do you know your teacher's name? (2)

Do you live in a house or a flat? (52)

Do you want milk and sugar?

Do you work in the evenings?

How many children does he have?

When does she go to bed? (212)

Your friend, John, has just introduced you to another friend of his, Peter. Use these frames to make questions you might ask Peter.

Where .... come from?   *When .... meet John?*
What work ....?   *Where ....?*
.... live?

Make questions from this table.

When What time	do does did	you Myf	start work? finish work? get up? go to bed? have lunch? get home in the evening?

2   used to make a verb negative

I don't go to work as such. (118)

I don't always have lunch actually. (113)

A: Do you know where Green Park is? B: No, I'm sorry, I don't.

I didn't do anything interesting.

I do not know yet whether I shall be staying with Vijay Bhatia. (193)

Do not insert money.

Say which of these things you do and which you don't do.

speak English / Italian / Spanish / German / French / Chinese / Japanese
play football / tennis / cricket / golf / chess
ride a bicycle
drive a car
fly a plane

---

3   used with a noun to show an activity

Can you do the table for me?

So you do your shopping by car.

I did quite a bit of shopping last weekend.

He did the meals when I was ill.

Then after lunch I did some shopping.

They have a design agency. They do leaflets and brochures. (24)

Wait a minute. I'll do that for you.

I would like to do another English course. (94)

I usually do two hours' work in the evenings.

I left home and went to London to do a secretarial course. (157)

Which person in your family:

does the cooking?   does the shopping?   does the car?
does the dishes?   does the cleaning?   does the table?

What jobs do you think children should do to help around the house?

---

4   to work (at a job or as a student)

What work do you do?

5   to be enough

I've got £5. Will that do?

6   'to do with' (meaning 'concerning')

... swimming, ski-ing, anything to do with sport. (98)

Is it anything to do with sport? (188)

7   for emphasis

I do remember meeting you.

7.1   as a very polite invitation

Do have another.

Do come and see us.

Do sit down.

for (93)

1   how long

He paused for a moment. (94)

Bridget lived in Sussex for some years before coming to London.

They are out for the afternoon.

Complete these to make true sentences.

I have been learning English I have lived in .... I went to Primary School I haven't had anything to eat I haven't had anything to drink	for ....

Say whether these sentences are true about you.

1 *Most years I go away on holiday for a week or so.*
2 *I usually watch TV for at least an hour in the evening.*
3 *Last week I watched TV for more than six hours altogether.*
4 *I often go away for the weekend.*
5 *I have had my present job for more than a year.*

1.1 when for

I have to finish this report for tomorrow.
Let's arrange a meeting for next week.

2 why

Look at these forms. What are they for? (14)
I've got six houses for sale. (72)
Learn the questions that are useful for your English
    lessons.
She was waiting for a friend. (93)
For example . . . (4)

2.1 'ask / look for'

Look at section 93 for more examples.
Ask four students for their names and phone
    numbers. (9)

3 who wants or needs . . .

Can you spell your name for me. (11)
This next record is for Pat Malone. (74)
Learn the questions that are useful for you in your
    English lessons.
Wait a minute. I'll do that for you.

3.1 after 'good/bad', 'easy/difficult', 'right'

It's good for you to take a lot of exercise.
I hope this won't be too difficult for you.

get, got (32, 116)

1 'get in / to / on / off' etc.

What floor does he get out of the lift on? (115)
What time do you get up? (118)
I get up at about seven. (113)
You get off at the junction. (125)
You get off the bus at the stop in the Bristol Road.
    (125)

2 'I've got . . .' (see have 1 and 2)

Have you got any brothers and sisters? (19)
Excuse me, have you got Liz's phone number? (31)
I haven't got a credit card. (25)
Have you got a garden? (52)
Haven't you got these in another colour? (102)
You must have got the wrong number. (210)

Make true sentences from this table.

I've got	a pen a book some coins a tissue a credit card a ruler some money	on my desk. in my pocket.

Make questions like this to ask your partner.

Have you got some coins in your pocket?

3 'I've got to . . .' (see have 4)

How many have we got to have? (70)
I've got to finish my work.

4 obtain / receive

I'm going to the bank to get some money.
Did you get my letter?
I ran after her to get my bag back.

5 turn / become

It gets very cold in winter.
He sometimes gets very angry.

go (159)

1 move / travel

Wherever you go during your holiday take a
    Phonecard along with you.
It's time to go.

1.1 'go to / out (of) / into / back (to)' etc.

Elsa wants to go to England to improve her spoken
    English. (82)
I have to go out at six thirty.
You'd have to go into the town.
It's after midnight before we go to bed. (113)
John didn't go to Manchester, so he must have gone
    to Birmingham. (158)
I walked past him to go back to the platform.

1.2 'go and . . .'

Shall we go and have a drink? (68)
I'll go and phone Smiths.

Make questions and answers from these tables.

Shall we Let's	go and	have a drink see a film play football have lunch watch television see George	. / ?

No thanks.	I've got to I have to	write some letters. go straight home. finish my work. do the cooking.

2 'go to' = attend

I'm going to a concert on Saturday night. (188)
Bridget's brother goes to Southampton University.
We are all going to a party tonight.

3 'go on' = continue

You go on another mile or so.

4 'going to' for future or intention

We're going to see a film after class. (100)
I'm going to learn English next term.

Make sentences about what you are going to do next week.

I'm going to	go to work on go shopping on go to the bank on watch TV on stay at home on	Monday. Tuesday. Wednesday. etc.

5 'go' does not have any meaning – it takes its meaning from the words that come after it (compare do 3)

go shopping	go for a game of	go for a walk
go swimming	go running / jogging	go for a drive
go for a swim	go for a run / jog	

have, had (32, 156)

1 possess (see get 2)

Jenny has a flat in North London. (24)
I don't have a watch. (25)

1.1 wear or carry with you

The man in my picture also has a brown hat. (38)
Amina has her book. (230)

What things do you have with you? Make sentences like:

I have	a some	———,	but I don't have	a any	———.

Use these ideas to help you.

pen	coins	diary	calculator	keys
pencil	money	notebook	credit card	

1.2 be related to or know someone

X is married and has two children. (18)
I have two brothers, one older and one younger. (26)

2 with a time (+ 'to') (see get 2)

I don't think I will have time to see you.
I may have time to show you the neighbourhood. (176)

3 food or drink

Have lunch with the family. (188)
I had to find out what time you had your meals. (143)
And you had tea there? with your aunt? (155)
Do you have a coffee break?

4 'have to' (see get 2)

I had to come down as the phone was ringing. (91)
I had to find out what time you had your meals. (143)
I have to book my tickets very soon. (176)
I'll have to go shopping at some stage. (188)
I've had to do it as cheaply as I could. (221)

Say whether you <u>have to</u> or <u>don't have to</u> do these things.

do the cooking	do the shopping	go to school
do the dishes	go to work	learn English

What about your mother / father or husband / wife?

5 'have' does not have any meaning – it takes its meaning from the words that come after it (compare <u>do</u> 3)

Did you have a look at the shops?
Let's have a game of football.
I'm going to have a rest.
Did you have a good sleep?

6 used to make present perfect tense ('have' + -ed / -en) –

6.1 when we are talking about the past but thinking about the present

I've never been to Spain. (171)
Do you want to summarise this one? Oh no, I've written it down. (140)
I've forgotten my book. (230)
The busiest day I've had recently was last Monday. (152)
Since my daughter, Becky, left to go to college I've had a few people staying. (163)

Look at the exercise under <u>for</u> 1.

Think of questions you might ask someone at home, at school, or at work.

Have you .... yet?

Here are some ideas to help you.

do the dishes	typing
washing	letters
table	your homework
the exercise	finish the dishes

Look at these sentences and match questions and answers.

1 *Where's Philip?*
2 *How about the film on TV?*
3 *Do you know London well?*
4 *Are you going home?*
5 *When are we going out?*
6 *Where's your watch?*

a *I've already seen it twice.*
b *No, I've never been there.*
c *As soon as I've written this letter.*
d *No. I haven't done all my work.*
e *I think I've lost it.*
f *He's gone out.*

Notice that the questions all refer to present time

Make sentences like:

I've ...., but I've never ....

Some ideas:

Have you ever played tennis / cricket / billiards / football / chess?
Have you ever visited London / Rome / Madrid / Tokyo / Britain / Italy / Spain / Japan?
Have you ever studied French / Chinese / Japanese / maths / history / astrology?

6.2 for something that will have happened at some time in the future

He'll be home when he's finished work.
Tell me when you've finished.
(We can also use the present tense.)
He'll be home when he finishes work.
Tell me when you finish.)*

Make answers to the question 'Can I go home early?'

Yes, you can go home	as soon as when
No, you can't go home	until

you've	finished done	the letters. this exercise. the typing.
you	finish do	your work. everything.

6.3 'had' + -ed / -en

The article and photo had been in the papers that morning.
Mr Smith had lost his suitcase and was looking everywhere for it. (198)
What did you do after you had graduated?

if (209)

1 in conditions

1.1 when the speaker thinks something is likely to happen.

What happens if the person isn't there?
It will help if you know where the hole or button is in your phone. (205)

1.2 for something imagined, not real (see <u>would</u> 2)

Which examples would be useful if you went to Britain?
If you were counting, how would you say these numbers? (79)

105

2 after 'know', 'ask', 'see', 'find out' etc.

I wonder if we went to the same places.
Let's see if we're right. (171)
See if you were right. (96)
Bob asks Charles if he lives in a house or a flat. (150)
(You can also use whether instead of if in any of these sentences.)

3 'as if'

It also looks to me as if it could be somewhere in
  Canada, again. (171)
He sounded as if he was very tired.

in (56)

1 where

Both his brothers live in England. (46)
Both my sisters live in London. (46)
Bob lives in a part of Birmingham called West Heath.
  (50)
Are they in the bedroom? (51)

1.1 for books, pictures, diagrams etc.

What colour shoes has the lady on the far left got in
  your picture? (38)
Say which is the keyword in each phrase. (40)

2 for groups of people

Stand in two groups. (38)
In all your families together, are there more men and
  boys or women and girls? (28)

3 when

It was built for newspaper owner William Randolph
  Hearst in 1922–39. (55)
In Britain it can be very cold in winter, especially in
  December and January.

3.1 after

In ten years' time, Birmingham will be very different.
  (94)
You can go now, but come back in ten minutes' time.

4 for languages

He has a lot of books. They are in different languages.
  (46)
All the small blue books are in French. (46)

5 'in fact'

-ing (213)

1 describing something

I've got a man wearing a hat.
There was a man carrying a brown bag.
You hear a ringing tone. (206)
A purring sound.

2 after 'am', 'is', 'be' etc.

At one o'clock I'm normally eating my lunch. (143)
They were walking past the newsagents.

3 after 'see', 'hear' etc.

If you heard someone shouting for help. (208)
He saw a woman lying on the floor. (210)

4 before 'am', 'is' etc.

Learning English is easy, difficult.
Watching TV is...

5 after 'stop', 'start', 'remember', 'like' etc.

He stopped talking and began to eat.

6 after 'when', 'before', 'instead of' etc.

Instead of putting your money in first, you dial the
  number... (206)
Can you use the cardphone without using coins?

is, are, am, was, were (8, 17, 29)

1 who, what

Who are these people? What are their surnames?
  (4)
There are more green triangles than black ones. (35)
How many things are there on the tray? (42)
The largest private house in the world is Biltmore
  House in Asheville, North Carolina, USA. (55)
The smallest house in Britain is a cottage in North
  Wales. (55)
All the people in the street are girls or women. (67)
Her husband is an engineer. (71)

2 what it is / was like, what kind it is / was

Bridget is English. (17)
What colour are the man's jeans? (33)
These ones are very nice.
What do you know about Napoleon? Do you think
  he was rich or poor?
Our house is very quiet at night. (120)
It's a red one.
Are you tired?

3 where (from)

She's from Sussex. (17)
They are all from Unit 1. (8)
Do you know where they're from? (2)
Below the bananas on the bottom left was a book.
  (42) *(see section 45, there)*

4 + -ing

The girl on the left is wearing a sort of orangey
  blouse. (36)
The man is carrying a brown bag. (38)
The man's carrying an umbrella. (70)
The cat is sitting on the right. (70)
She was waiting for a friend. (93)
A lot of people are looking for houses in this area. (97)
What are you doing this summer?
Are you coming to the film?
What are you looking at? (120)
He was driving at eighty miles an hour.

5 + -ed / -en

Your father's called John? and your mother's called
  Pat? (19)
It was built in 1890. (55)
It was built for William Randolph Hearst. (55)
This street is called Montague Street Precinct. (67)
...teenage girls who are interested in fashion... (95)
Are you tired?
Wally is awakened by the phone ringing. (91)
...so that I can make sure that you are properly
  looked after. (193)
Listen for the words that are stressed. (103)

Which categories do these examples belong to?

1 *David's surname is Foll.*
2 *She's six.*
3 *She's at school.*
4 *He's called David.*
5 *My father's name was John.*
6 *She's from Sussex.*
7 *It's a small flat but it's near the shops.*

Look at these questions.

Was she carrying a bag? *What are their names?*
Was it nice? *Where is the black square?*
Is she married?

Put these words in the right order to make questions.

1 *David is who Foll*
2 *a Bridget secretary is*
3 *flat is David's in London*
4 *surname is Bridget's what*
5 *the woman what was carrying*
6 *Bridget's is flat where*

it (63, 88, 220)

1 pointing back

BG: Can I have your address? DF: Yeah. Okay. So
   it's twenty-one... (10)
What sort of house or flat do you live in? Is it big or
   small? (50)
Bridget lives in a big flat. It has two bedrooms. (52)

2 pointing forward

It's better to learn to swim and ride a bike while
   you're young. (107)
Didn't you find it difficult living in London by
   yourself?
It's always fun to watch the races.
It's quicker, cheaper and easier when you can dial
   direct. (206)

Make true sentences from this table.

It's	easy difficult fun interesting boring	learning English. to learn English. going to parties. to go to a party. when you meet new people.

3 for time, weather etc.

What time is it in Rio de Janeiro? (90)
By then it's about 7.15 or 7.30 p.m.
There is absolutely nothing to do when it rains.
Bring lots of jumpers as it could be quite cold. (176)
Lovely day, isn't it? (232)
It doesn't matter. (136)
It will be a fairly busy time for us on the farm. (176)

4 for an unknown person

Who was it on the phone? Was it a man or a woman?

of (17, 139)

1 used in expressions of quantity, size etc.

I've got one of those. (25)
Neither of your brothers. (26)
Where's that bit of paper? (107)
None of the yellow shapes are squares. (35)
He talked to a lot of other people. (107)
I did quite a bit of work last weekend.
Bring lots of jumpers. (176)

1.2 containing / consisting of something

Here are two sets of examples.
Let's find a place to have a cup of coffee.

1.3 'part of', 'some of' etc.

The middle of the morning. (84)
Tell the rest of the class. (106)
Tell each other your half of the story. (115)
The end of Saint Laurence Road. (125)

2 belonging to

Do you know the names of the students in your class?
   (2)
David tried to remember the names of Bridget's
   family. (19)
The number of a house. (77)
What's the name of the college? (109)

3 'sort of' etc.

3.1 spoken only – used to show the speaker doesn't want to sound very exact; or used instead of a pause or hesitation

The watch is sort of next to the glass of water. (42)
We sort of get on well. (53)

3.2

That sort of roof? (171)
Three types of telephone. (206)

4 dates, times, ages

My father is the first of May. (81)
At the age of 18.
End of July.

so (200)

1 marking a summary or a change of subject

Okay. So we've got the camel in the sunset next.
   (171)
So what do you do at quarter to eight? (143)
Right. So Mary went to London. (158)

2 expressing amount

There are always so many tourists.
No wonder you look so tired. (142)

3 meaning 'therefore'

The suitcase looked exactly like mine, so I said
   'Excuse me, sir...'

4 pointing back

JV: Wouldn't you think Cairo was 1500? DL: Yes,
   out of the ones given, I would've thought so. (90)

5 'so that' used to talk about result or purpose

It had a thick lining, so that you could practically
   sleep out in it. (104)
Let me know as soon as you have fixed your travel
   plans, so that I can make sure that you are properly
   looked after. (193)

6 meaning 'also'

JV: The woman next to him has orange
   trousers. DL: So has mine. (38)
David lives in London and so does Bridget.

Look at these examples.

I'm tired.	So am I / So is she.
I've finished.	So have I / So has she.
I'll help.	So will I / So will she.
I like it.	So do I / So does she.
I liked it.	So did I / So did she.

Reply to these sentences in the same way.

1 *I'm hungry.*
2 *I enjoyed the film.*
3 *He always comes.*
4 *They're going home.*
5 *She's done it before.*
6 *He'll have to work harder.*
7 *She was so tired she went straight to sleep.*

that (168)

1 pointing back (compare it, section 63)

That would be nice. (119)
So we did that one first. That was the easy one. (158)
You took them shopping. Then after that you went to visit an aunt, nearby. (155)

2 that person / thing

So we did that one first. (158)
I know all the people that worked on that magazine. (146)
Yes. That map's just right. (127)

(With meanings 1 and 2 'that' is pronounced /ðæt/.)

3 after 'say', 'know', 'hope', 'think' etc.

Most people think that Britain is too cold to grow grapes. (179)
I'm absolutely positive that that's New York. (171)
I didn't realise that it was an old briefcase of mine.

4 'so that' for purpose / result

It had a thick lining, so that you could practically sleep out in it. (104)
Let me know as soon as you have fixed your travel plans, so that I can make sure that you are properly looked after. (193)

5 defining thing(s) / people etc.

Listen for the words that are stressed. (103)
I know all the people that work on that magazine. (146)
Choose two places on the map that are quite close. (129)
There's a bus route that goes near his home from the University.

(With meanings 3, 4 and 5, 'that' is nearly always pronounced /ðət/. Often it is left out altogether. For category 5 we can use 'who' (for people) or 'which' (for things) instead of 'that'.)

Give the names of these people in your class.

Someone that / who	sits next to you. works hard. lives near you. smiles a lot. makes you laugh.

---

the (63, 235)

1 you know which one the speaker or writer means —

1.1 because they tell you which one

Do you know the names of the students in your class? (2)
Biltmore House is the biggest house in the world.
The man in the middle of the picture has blue trousers. (38)

1.2 because there is only one

the sun   the world

1.3 because there is only one around

the kitchen   the queen
the prime minister   the telephone

2 instead of a possessive like 'my', 'his', 'her', 'their' etc.

I have left my book in the office.

3 referring to a whole group of people or things

The Romans grew grapes in Britain.
The young should care for the old.

to (101, 150)

1 where

The yellow one is to the left of the red one. (34)
One of them went to Birmingham, one to Manchester and one to London. (158)
One of them went to the theatre. (158)
I went down to Sussex.
I will be travelling to Singapore from Kuala Lumpur.
I am sure you would enjoy a visit to Hawaii.

2 who (with 'give', 'offer', 'present' etc.)

Give your sentences to other students to read. (55)

3 listen or speak to someone / something

Kathryn Brown talked to Mrs Williams.
One child said to another. (165)
Tim called out to the woman but she didn't hear.

4 purpose

Give your sentences to other students to read. (55)
One of them went to London to visit her mother. (158)
So I chased him to get my suitcase back.

5 after 'ask', 'want', 'plan' etc.

How much money do I need to bring? (100)
I'm planning to buy something expensive. (101)
I would love to see you again.
I think we're going to be staying most of the time in Monze. (221)
Do you want to come with us? (100)

6 after 'it' (see it 2, section 88)

It's easy to eat it. (83)
It's better to learn to swim and ride a bike when you're young. (107)
It's better not to start smoking. (107)

7 after 'place', 'way', 'thing' etc.

What's the best way to do this?
What's the best thing to do now?
London is a good place to live.

8 from ... to ...

We lived in Birmingham from 1978 to 1980.
Prices range from £5.50 to £15.75.

9 used to, have (got) to, going to etc.

We're going to go on safari. (15)
You don't have to pay. (14)
You don't need to pay. (14)

Name a place in your country that is:

a good place to live.
an interesting place to visit.
a boring place to live.

---

wh- words (48, 141)

1 'when', 'where', 'which'

at the time when... in the place where... the thing which...

'when'

I left school when I was eighteen and went to university.

When Bridget left school she went to London to do a secretarial course.

When I left there, I started working for... (133)

When I see a windmill, I always think of Holland. (171)

It would be lovely to see you when you are in Britain. (176)

A man was walking down the street when he passed a woman carrying a suitcase... (198)

When you put your money in, there is a little reading... (206)

So I suppose the best time to phone is when she comes back from work. (211)

...but it's quicker, cheaper and easier when you can dial direct, especially from a British Telecom payphone. (206)

'where'

I started primary school at the age of almost four, at a private school in the Isle of Wight, where my father was working. (133)

I started working for Macmillan's publishers where I stayed for one and a half years. (133)

DF: Are you planning to stay where you are? BG: For the time being. Yes. (191)

The new ones are the ones where you just press a button to dial the number.

'which'

David's best buy was a United States Air Force overcoat, which was reduced in price from £25 to £5. (104)

Bridget bought a big man's jumper which started off at about £7.

...a ferry called Queensferry... which took cars and people across the river... (179)

I live in the country which is very muddy. (176)

I'm going out to lunch in Putney, which is close-ish. (188)

There are two types of phones. The older type which are the dial phones, and the more recent type which are the press-button phones. (206)

So, at about 5.45 her time, which is 1.45 our time. (212)

Complete these sentences with a clause with 'where', 'when', 'which' (or 'that') or 'who'.

1 *I know a nice shop .... you can buy ....*
2 *I left school .... I was ....*
3 *Then I went to ...., ... I stayed for .... months / years.*
4 *The best bargain I ever got was a ...., ... I / was ....*
5 *We're going out to a restaurant .... is not too far from here, and where the food ....*
6 *I know the people .... work there, so we always get very good food, ... is nice.*
7 *.............. I got home, I found a lot of letters by the door.*

---

2 'when', 'where', 'which', 'what', 'who', 'how', 'why'

2.1 after 'tell', 'know', 'ask', 'remember' etc.

Do you know where they're from? (2)

Can you tell me how to get to your house from the bus stop?

Can you remember where she lives?

Can you tell me what we have to do?

Do you know how to make a phone call in Britain?

Tell me when you are free. (176)

Let me know when you plan to arrive.

2.2 in questions

What's the best time to phone?

What do you think will happen next?

What sort of people would buy each magazine? (95)

What time do you go to bed? (142)

Where did you live before? (57)

Which room do you think is the nicest? (51)

When's your birthday? (81)

When will you be arriving?

How do you say your name in your country? (5)

How many children have you got?

A: How far is it? B: Two miles. A: How long by bus? B: 15 minutes.

BG: I don't like that. DF: Why not? (96)

Who do you work for?

2.3 more questions with 'who'

Who goes to bed latest?

Who works longer hours?

Who's going to write the list?

Look at these questions.

Who does Bridget work for?
Bridget works for Collins.

Who did you see at the party?
We saw Richard at the party.

Who's the easiest person to contact at home?
Bridget's the easiest person to contact at home.

Who lives here?
Danny lives here.

2.4 'what happens'

What happens if the person isn't there?

will, would (94, 174)

(See if 1.2.)

1 for fact or prediction

Chicago will be 7 a.m., wouldn't it? (90)

You will hear Myf interviewing either Philip or Ken. (109)

It will be my first time in Britain. (12)

This evening if you come home tomorrow I won't be here. (199)

I will be travelling to Singapore from Kuala Lumpur.

In some areas you will find green cardphones. (205)

What do you think the weather will be like next week?

Will it be warm / hot / cool / cold / freezing / wet / dry?
Will it rain / snow?

What will you be doing:

at six o'clock this evening?
this time tomorrow?
this time next week?

2 for something imagined, not real ('would')

Imagine that you would be very happy to see the
person.

What do you think the weather would be like if you were:

in London?   in Rome?   in Madrid?   in Moscow?
in Cairo?

If you were asked to make a film:

what book or play would you choose?
who would the stars be?
what parts would they play?

**Suppose an English friend asked you what to do and what
places to visit in your country. What would you tell them?**

**If you wanted to save money, which of these things would
you do?**

Eat less?
Drink less?
Spend less on going out?
Sell your car?
Spend less on clothes?

---

3 to make an offer or announce a decision or promise

I'll be back home at twelve.
I promised I'd be back home at twelve.

('Would' is the past tense of 'will'.)

What might you say if you:

promised you would be home early?
promised you wouldn't stay out late?
promised to help someone?
offered to carry someone's bag?
offered to give someone a lift?
decided to take a taxi home?
decided to walk home?

3.1 to make a request

Will you do it?
Will you help me?

4 'would like' = want

I would like to visit your part of Britain.
I would love to see you again.
We're going to the cinema. Would you like to come?

Name three countries you would like to visit.
Name three famous people you would like to meet.
Name three famous people you wouldn't like to meet.

---

with (99, 204)

1 together with

I've come to Liverpool to stay with my parents. (98)
Discuss with your partner. (78)
I worked with her a long time ago.

2 used to describe things or people

It was very very big, in very good condition with a
thick lining. (104)
How many expressions can you hear with 'think' or
'thought'? (92)
A shirt with no buttons. (38)

3 how

Something you're not going to actually work with.
Your friends need a watch to time you with.

Wordlist

Words in **bold** type are explained in the Grammar Book on pages 101–110. Figures refer to sections where good examples of the words are given in context, either in the Students Book or in the transcripts where marked with an asterisk. Figures in **bold** type refer to sections where explanation are given.
(T) after a reference means your teacher will give you the word to help you with this section.

a **32, 63**, 151
able 108, **121**
about 19, **27**, 80
above 193, **204**
across 127*, **139**
actually 113, 155, **236**
address 10
afraid 113, 198, **204**
Africa 170
after **94**
afternoon 84(T)
again 17m, 198
age **46**
ago **94**
agree 96
air 221, **236**
alive **96, 181**
all 35, 48c, 225, 230, **236**
almost 80
alone 66
along **124, 139**
already **139**
also 63, 104
always 171*
am 2, 188*, 190, 191*, 193
America 170
American 79, 181
an **32, 63**
and 5, 17, 73, 204c
another 37, 102, **107**, 139
answer, answered 53, 210
any 19, 27, **121**
anyone **121, 150**
anything **121**
anyway 119
April 81
are **8, 17j**
arm 38
army 74c
arrangement 193
arrive, arrived 193
as 76d³, **177**
ask, asked 5, 25
at **120, 164**
August 81
autumn 175
available 205
away 125*, 139g
baby, babies 18
back 58, 225, 232
bad 104
bag 36
bank 108
be **93, 192, 193**
because 41
become, became, become 46, 116
bed 51
been **202**
before **94**
begin, begun, began 109, **150**
behind 122
bell 173
below 104
best 66, 77, 84, 107
better 57, **107**
between 34, **124**
big 18, 164
birth 81
bit 107
black 34
blue 34
body, bodies 48(T)
book 1(T), 46, 204c
born 69
borrow, borrowed 65
both 23, **32, 48, 204**

bottom 171*c
boy 18
bring, brought 61, **236**
Britain 175
British 179, 181
brother 18
brown 36
building 49
bus 77, 79
business 151
busy 151
but 25*, 73, 221, 230
buy, bought 95, 104
by **111**
call, called 20
can 11, **138, 183, 220b**
car 40
carefully 28
carry, carried 38(T)*
cent 104
centre 123
century, centuries 179
certain 93
certainly 89, **236**
chair 51(T), 131
chance 225
change, changed 83
cheap 98
check, checked 125
child, children 18, 60
church 122
city, cities 123
class 2
close, closed 51, 72, 81, 123
clothes 39
coast 179
coffee 47, 108
cold 176, 179
college 109
colour 33
come, came, come 16, 17n, 199, **204a**
common 62, 66, 138
compare 60
corner 125
cost 55
could **93, 138, 183, 220b**
country 155, 170
couple 127*
course **48, 82**
cross, crossed 127*
daily 216
dark 37, 205
date 77, 78
daughter 18(T), 19
day 17, 81
dead 181
December 84
decide, decided 140, 171
definitely 90*, 93*
degree 175(T)
desk 72*
detail 185
dialogue 31
did 57, 59, **183**
difference 36
different 7
difficult **84***
dinner 113
direction 122, 217
do 50, **59, 132, 183, 204**
doctor 74
door 52(T)
double 91
down **139**
drink, drank, drunk 68
drive, drove, driven 155

during 121, 206
each 84
early 113
east **66**
easy 86
eat, ate, eaten 67
education 133
eight **6**
either **6**
eleven **6**
else 115(T), **121**
emergency 205
end 125, **150**
England 82
English 3, 14, 82
enjoy, enjoyed 98
enough **150**
entrance 122
especially 206
Europe 171
even 175, **186**
evening 84, 94f
ever 76
every 99
everyone 113, 121
everything 121, 150a
exact 80
exactly 139
examination 82
example 4
except 82, **94**
expensive 55
experience 176
eye 37
face 48(T)
fact 127*, **236**
family, families 18
famous 74c
far 123, 125
farm 176
fashionable 96
father 18(T), 19
February 81
feel, felt 87, 107
few 146
fifteen 79
fifty, fifties 79
figure 232
find, found 19, 21, 24
fine 65, 176, 179
finish, finished 21, 150
fire 205
first 5, 6, 11, 206
five 6
flat 49, 171*a
floor 49, 54, 115
food 67
foot 38(T)
for **93**
forest 179
forget, forgot, forgotten 42
form, formed 14, 125*, 133, 163
forty, forties 79
forward 82, **204**
four 6
fourteen 79
France 170
Free 205
French 46
Friday 17
friend 17
from 2, **124**, 236d
front 58
full 84, 203
furniture 51(T)
further 125, **139**
future 190, 191, **204**
game 42
garden 57
general 82
get, got 20, 27, 32, 53, **116, 156**
girl 18(T), 19
give, gave, given 104, 122
glass, glasses 42, 140

go, went, gone, going 71, 133, 159, 196b, 203, **223**
good 107
goodbye 1
government 169
great 74c, 188*
green 34
grey 36
ground 115
group 38
had 25, **156, 231**
hair 36, 96
half, halves 84(T), 152*b
hall 52*
hand 48(T)
happen, happened 173
hard 108
hat 38*
have 20, 27, 32b, 156, 183, 195, 205, **220**
he 2, 4
head 48
hear, heard 206, 210
hello 1, 215
help, helped 208, 220
her 2, 17, **32, 48**
here **171***, **186**
herself **144**
high 170
hill 185
him 38*, 48
himself **144**
his **4, 17f, 32f**
history 179
hold, held 38, 89
holiday 233
home 50, 113, **157**
hope, hoped 233, **236**
hospital 122
hot 175(T)
hour 84
house **49**, 50, 55
how 22, 36, 48, 134, **141**
however 225
hundred 78
husband 18(T), 22
I 2
idea 185
if **208, 209**
ill 74
important 152, 163
in 56, 82, **124, 236**
individual 82
information 82
inside 72*, 76e, **204**
instead **143, 150, 236**
instruction 205
interest, interested 95, 160
into 125*, **186**
is **8, 17j**, 74, **183**
it 21, 63, 88, **220**
its 49
itself 144T
January 81
job 108
July 81
June 81
just 80, 122, 150
keep, kept **218**
key 23, 74
kitchen 51
kind 95
know, knew, known 2, 4, 17, **186**
labour 161, 163
lady 38T
language 46
large 40, 46
last 87, **94**
late 113
later 173
law 151
learn, learnt/learned 14
leave, left 108, 118
left 34

111